I Do!

I Do!

A MARRIAGE WORKBOOK
FOR ENGAGED COUPLES

JIM WALKUP, LMFT

ALTHEA
PRESS

For general information on our other products and services or to obtain technical support, please contact our Customer Care Department within the U.S. at (866) 744-2665, or outside the U.S. at (510) 253-0500.

Althea Press publishes its books in a variety of electronic and print formats. Some content that appears in print may not be available in electronic books, and vice versa.

Interior Designer: Carol Angstadt
Cover Designer: Amy King
Editor: Susan Randol
Production Editor: Andrew Yackira
Author photo: © OSullivanStudios.com

ISBN: Print 978-1-64152-213-7 | eBook 978-1-64152-214-4

To Betsy, my dear wife of 49 years, who believed so much in this book that she became the wind behind my sails. Our relationship gave us an opportunity to discover many insights that you will find in this workbook. By searching for what would work, we have built a marriage that has given me much joy and meaning. Her love and support have blessed me throughout our life together.

Contents

INTRODUCTION
Let's Begin

SO YOU'RE ENGAGED TO get married—congratulations! Chances are you've announced your engagement to your friends and family, and maybe you've even started planning your wedding. When you look back years from now, this time will likely stand out as one of the most exciting periods of your life. Many steps lie ahead for you as you cross the bridge from engagement to walking down the aisle. Every step you take will bring you closer to your goal of having a happy and satisfying marriage. This workbook is one of those steps, and it may very well be one of the most important steps you'll take together between now and then.

I grew up in a family of ministers and always thought I'd become one, but halfway through seminary, I realized I didn't want to preach sermons every Sunday. So, instead, I studied to become a marriage counselor. While I was at seminary I met Betsy. We fell in love, and I soon started thinking about asking her to marry me. Like many couples, we had our differences, which concerned me. Betsy did not enjoy spending as much time with people as I did. She was a bottom-line person, whereas I tended to follow my intuition. She thrived on making plans and working toward them, but I preferred to be more spontaneous.

One day I told Betsy that I wouldn't marry anyone who hadn't engaged in some counseling, and she promptly broke up with me. Fortunately, a couple of weeks later, she called a counselor, and we began therapy together. Betsy and I give that decision partial credit for our satisfying 49 years of marriage. In fact, a 2003 study published in *Family Relations* indicates that couples who engage in some form of premarital counseling have 30 percent higher marital satisfaction than those who do not. You're smart to take the time to get a head start on building your marriage before it even starts.

As a New York State–licensed therapist for more than 40 years, I have helped hundreds of couples find solid ground on which to build their relationships. Teaching them the skills and tools to grow their love and strengthen their partnerships has served as one of the principal joys of my life. The topics covered in this book are those that the couples in my premarital counseling sessions typically explore, so you will likely relate.

In this workbook you will begin to anticipate and master some of the sticking points couples experience before they say, "I do!" As you read the discussions and do the exercises together, you will gain insights, tips, and tools to strengthen your bond and head into your marriage with as robust a relationship as possible. In working and playing together throughout this workbook you will learn many new things about each other. Some of those things may surprise you. You may even discover that you have some differences you didn't know about. That's okay. You will learn ways to merge your similarities and differences to build a stable relationship that will keep you feeling close and connected.

No matter your background or situation, this workbook can help as you move forward in your relationship with confidence. *I Do!* addresses a variety of premarital situations:

- You recently met and got engaged right away. You are excited to learn the principles of building a great relationship.
- You have been together for a few years and want to do all you can to make sure you know how to make your relationship last.
- One or both of you were married before, and you want to go into this marriage wiser from the past experience.

- You come from different backgrounds and want to create the strongest bridge possible to connect your different worlds.
- You've encountered a few problems and want tips and tools to solve them so that you can walk confidently down the aisle.

Explore the chapters in order of interest or approach them in consecutive order but complete them all. The most important part of this process is that you read the discussions and do the exercises together as a couple. Carve out time on a regular basis to work on this book together. Spend at least a week on each chapter. There are nine chapters here, so plan accordingly so that you will have ample time to complete all the exercises before your wedding.

Throughout the chapters, you will find questions, prompts, and more to stimulate your thinking with space for each of you to respond. Choose which of you will be "partner A" and "partner B" (flip a coin if you can't decide). The person designated "partner A" doesn't always have to tackle the exercises first; take turns going first. Also take turns reading the discussions aloud to each other. Jot down some notes following your discussions to record ideas, compromises, strategies, agreements, and more.

Explore this workbook and yourselves with gusto! Take as long as you need to discuss your responses to the exercises. Both of you need to engage in this process for success. After quiet personal reading and reflection, always share with your partner what you have learned and what you intend to do as a result. Talking over these topics and putting the suggestions into practice will help you develop the habits to communicate easily, resolve conflict, and create a meaningful future together. At the end of each chapter, you will have opportunities to reflect on what strikes you as useful and explore some fun ways to put what you've learned into action.

You may feel awkward at first when you try some of these approaches. Feel free to be a bit playful as you practice something new. When it becomes second nature to communicate and interact in meaningful ways, you will reap the rewards of being a team and taking on the world together.

CHAPTER

1

Strengthen Your Bond and Your Commitment

COUPLES WHO PARTICIPATE IN premarital counseling achieve a statistically lower chance of divorce, according to research cited by the American Psychological Association. This is because they are investing their time in building a strong foundation for their relationship moving forward. With this workbook in hand, that's what you're doing: starting off on the right foot by learning what you can do to build a deep and lasting bond. Just as you are taking steps to create the wedding of your dreams, you are now taking steps to create a marriage that will last a lifetime.

With today's fast-paced, technology-driven lifestyles, there can be a lot of pressure steering you away from investing time in each other. I commend you on making the decision to put away all the distractions to devote time to this process. As you make your way through this workbook, focus on opening the lines of communication and addressing potential problems early on with the ultimate goal of building a strong foundation for your marriage.

THE BENEFITS

Throughout this workbook, you will be examining how you grew up and how you see things today, and exploring your views on important marriage-related topics. This is a lot like putting your relationship under a microscope. When you open up the lines of communication, you'll see everything up close and personal—and that's the point. You will learn the art of talking to each other openly and respectfully, even when you disagree. Sharing your perspective is the key to getting to know each other really well and developing a lifelong rapport. In addition to learning the art of communicating, here are the many benefits of exploring what makes you both tick and finding common ground.

Learn Conflict Resolution Skills

Every couple experiences conflicts. However, by working on the skills in this book, you will develop a caring style of hearing each other when you are at odds. You will learn that underneath anger lies a yearning to be heard, cared about, and respected. Listening for that longing will make the difference between an angry confrontation and a peaceful resolution.

Develop Realistic Expectations

You come to your engagement with expectations that may at times fall short of what is likely to happen. Fairy tales talk about living happily ever after, but that's only if you have learned to take a long, loving look at reality and deal with it. When you pause to listen to your inner sense of the truth about what's before you, you will feel less reactive and be able to reach out with compassion.

Identify Potential (Common) Marital Problems

As you begin your life together, you may feel delighted that so far you are encountering only a few issues. Enjoy this stage of your engagement while using this workbook to anticipate the typical complications that occur in most marriages. You will find ways to develop the habits to deal with relationship challenges.

Get on the Same Page

Heading off in different directions will not serve you well. By mapping out a vision of your individual dreams, you can blend them together into a beautiful mosaic. In business, people with different temperaments need to build a team. In the same way, you will develop the skill of joining together and pulling your oars in sync.

RELATIONSHIP GROUND RULES

Having to follow "rules" probably doesn't sound like a fun way to start a life together, but there are rules for just about everything when we really think about it. Some of them are just common sense or common courtesy—and that's a lot like these suggested rules. It's essential that you both agree to follow the relationship rules you establish together. You can start with these, modify them as you see fit, and add a few of your own:

1. We promise to treat each other with respect. If we feel disrespected, we will ask our partner for a different approach.
2. We will set time for each other on a daily basis to catch up on our lives.
3. We will not let unfinished arguments linger. After a pause, we will follow up with each other to resolve hurt feelings.
4. We commit to being honest with each other.
5. We will allow each other to change and grow.
6. We will honor the aspects of privacy we have agreed upon.
7. We will not put each other down in public.
8. _____
9. _____
10. _____
11. _____
12. _____

Can you each agree on these relationship rules? Are there any you think you might have trouble following? Discuss any concerns you have and brainstorm ways you can get on the same page. If you're having a little trouble here, don't worry. As you do the exercises and learn more about each other's preferences, expectations, and hopes, you'll learn ways to honor your commitment to follow the relationship rules you've established together.

Exploring your innermost feelings and learning about each other will help you attain a level of intimacy that many couples never achieve. Having the courage to explore your strengths and your vulnerabilities will draw you nearer to each other. As you do so, you will be amazed at how your commitment as a couple grows. You will want to protect and support each other because you see and admire the heart and the soul of your partner.

MARRIAGE MYTHS

Couples heading into marriage may believe they know what lies ahead. Their assumptions are often based on relationships they have seen depicted in books, movies and on television, or heard about from friends and family. But much of what newly engaged couples assume about marriage isn't really true. As a couple, read the following statements and see if you can identify which are myths:

1. Married couples should know what the other person needs without having to ask or tell them.
2. If two people discover that they are very different, they probably shouldn't have gotten married.
3. Married people never feel lonely.
4. When a couple has children, they grow closer.
5. Married couples have less sex than they did before they got married or after the honeymoon phase.
6. If a couple really loves each other, they won't fight that much.
7. When a couple gets married, life always flows more smoothly.
8. Married couples should do just about everything together.
9. After the honeymoon period, being married will become boring.
10. Getting married "completes" you.

You probably guessed that all of these statements are false, but did any of them ring true to you? For example, do you buy into the idea that once you get married, your sex life will eventually become humdrum? Or perhaps you think that "I do!" really means "I don't have to worry about anything anymore because life from now on will be blissful."

Discuss each of these myths as a couple. Explore with each other why you might think one or more of these statements is even partly true, and then turn them inside out. For example, if you believe that two partners who really love each other shouldn't fight, remind yourself that even couples who love each other have arguments and will disagree occasionally (or maybe even frequently).

Discussion Notes

_____

_____

_____

_____

_____

THE PAST AND THE PRESENT

Every person enters into a marriage with preconceptions. These preconceptions are based on their exposure to their family of origin. Are you aware of your preconceptions—what you are bringing from your past into your present? By watching and learning from the adults in your life as you grew up, you have each learned things about marriage and family like:

- What it means to be male or female as it relates to marriage.
- Approaches for dealing with conflict with your partner.
- Models for loving your partner and expressing affection.
- Ways to handle the business end of life.

If you and your partner grew up in different cultures, you may have traditions and expectations of each other's roles in the marriage that seem reasonable to you but partially or completely unreasonable to your partner. You may not even be aware of these differences until you encounter your partner's approach *after* you're married. That's why it's so important to make every effort to approach potential differences with your partner now. Be curious.

This exercise gives you the chance to explore what formed your preconceptions of marriage and the roles each person plays in the partnership. After you have each responded fully to the prompts, there will be an opportunity for a discussion.

PARTNER A

Who were your male role models in your home and what were some of their identifying characteristics and behaviors?

_____

_____

_____

Who were your female role models in your home and what were some of their identifying characteristics and behaviors?

_____

_____

_____

How did your parents interact with each other? For example, were they affectionate in front of you? Did they treat each other with respect? Did they socialize together or did they spend a lot of time apart with their individual friends or alone?

_____

_____

_____

How did your parents deal with conflict? Did they argue or disagree a lot on everyday things? Were they often quiet and sullen if problems arose? Did they work well together to resolve issues?

_____

_____

_____

Who took care of the finances in your home? Who did the cleaning? Who did the cooking? Did one or both of your parents work? Who made the big decisions and purchases? Who was in charge of the social calendar?

_____

_____

_____

Who were your male role models in your home and what were some of their identifying characteristics and behaviors?

_____

_____

_____

Who were your female role models in your home and what were some of their identifying characteristics and behaviors?

_____

_____

_____

How did your parents interact with each other? For example, were they affectionate in front of you? Did they treat each other with respect? Did they socialize together or did they spend a lot of time apart with their individual friends or alone?

_____

_____

_____

How did your parents deal with conflict? Did they argue or disagree a lot on everyday things? Were they often quiet and sullen if problems arose? Did they work well together to resolve issues?

_____

_____

_____

Who took care of the finances in your home? Who did the cleaning? Who did the cooking? Did one or both of your parents work? Who made the big decisions and purchases? Who was in charge of the social calendar?

_____

_____

_____

Partner Discussion

Explore the similarities and differences you just uncovered. Go back and, as a couple, underline anything you think will work in your marriage. For example, did one or both sets of your parents equally share in the decision-making? Is that something you can both ascribe to? If so, underline it or use a highlighter so that it really stands out. Likewise, is there anything you learned growing up that could cause a potential conflict? For example, did one partner's parents fall into traditional male and female roles while the other partner's parents were a little looser? Discuss whether those perceptions have resulted in any expectations and if there's room to approach the roles differently. Brainstorm how you can use your different experiences growing up to blossom as a couple.

Discussion Notes

_____

_____

_____

_____

SETTING GOALS

You know the old saying, "If you don't know where you are going, you will probably wind up someplace else." If you haven't heard your partner articulate their dreams of what a beautiful marriage would look like and vice versa, you won't necessarily be working together toward the same shared future. So take this time to get concrete and specific about the future you want to create.

Marriage comes in many shapes and sizes. You get where you want to go by forming your vision together and intentionally taking the daily steps to make it happen. What will give you a sense that you are growing into the couple you want to be?

SET GOALS—YOURS, MINE, AND OURS

This worksheet includes a list of marriage goals (there's room to add a few of your own if you don't see them here). Each partner will have an opportunity to identify whether or not a goal is important to them personally. If a goal is important to you, rank its importance on a scale from 1 (low) to 5 (high). If it's not important to you at all, place an X in that row. You'll have an opportunity to discuss these goals with each other after you've both completed the exercise.

GOALS	PARTNER A	PARTNER B
ATTEND CULTURAL EVENTS		
BE EACH OTHER'S CHEERLEADER		
BUILD A FAMILY		
CULTIVATE PERSONAL/ARTISTIC TALENTS		
GET TOGETHER WITH RELATIVES		
HAVE ACCESS TO GOOD SCHOOLS		
MAINTAIN AN OPEN, HONEST RELATIONSHIP		
OBTAIN FINANCIAL SECURITY		
OWN A BEAUTIFUL HOME		
PARTICIPATE IN A SPIRITUAL OR RELIGIOUS COMMUNITY		
PURSUE FURTHER EDUCATION		
SOCIALIZE WITH FRIENDS		
PARTICIPATE IN SPORTS OR SPECTATORSHIP		
STAY IN GOOD PHYSICAL SHAPE		
TRAVEL		

ADD YOUR OWN	PARTNER A	PARTNER B

Partner Discussion

See where your goals match up or closely match up in importance. You can work toward those goals together by exploring how you will join each other in making that vision a reality. Perhaps you and your partner will have a few different goals. For example, maybe one of you wants to further your education and the other wants to pursue their artistic talents. In cases like that, you can plan on how to support each other's efforts.

If you have some glaring differences, discuss why a goal is or isn't important to one of you; this may open up new ways of thinking. Brainstorm ways to work through those differences and find a way to identify mutual goals that more closely align with what each of you envisions for a fulfilling marriage and life.

Discussion Notes

_____

_____

_____

_____

_____

MAKING THE COMMITMENT

When you make a commitment, you are giving your word to someone that you will do something. You can commit to little things like walking a neighbor's dog or to big things like taking a new job and doing your best work. Making a lifelong commitment to your partner in marriage, though, is among the most significant commitments you will make in life. But what does the word commitment mean to each of you and what does it mean to make a commitment to each other?

Many cultures view marriage as a sacred union and the commitment made to each other as divine law. Define for yourselves what it means to you as a couple to join as one while still maintaining your individuality. During your wedding ceremony, you will be making this commitment to each other with an intention of following through on your commitment for the rest of your lives.

Some couples write their own wedding vows while others use the traditional vows. Regardless of your preference, begin now to identify what you mean when you say, "I do." Don't underestimate the power of the marriage ritual to help you begin a beautiful life together.

FORMULATE YOUR PROMISES

Take a few minutes to think about what you are promising your partner when you say "I do" at your wedding ceremony. You can brainstorm on scrap paper, and then write your commitments in the space provided. If you are writing your own vows, this can be a good start to figure out what you want to say to each other on your wedding day.

> PARTNER A <

_____

_____

_____

_____

_____

> PARTNER B <

_____

_____

_____

_____

_____

Partner Discussion

Read each other's responses and discuss how your partner's promises make you feel. You should feel free to add to or revise your responses following this discussion. Remember, this is all about learning from each other. Be sure to revisit these commitments on a regular basis, before and after your wedding. (Be sure to record your vows at your wedding so you can listen to them on your anniversaries.)

Discussion Notes

CHAPTER

Communication: The Oxygen in Your Relationship

CAN YOU GUESS THE request I hear most often from couples who come to me for premarital counseling? They usually say, "Teach us how to communicate better." And I'm glad they do, because in marriage, good communication is key. In this chapter, you'll learn various strategies to help you share your thoughts and explore what's on your mind in a way that will encourage your partner to listen and share their own thoughts.

Communication takes many forms—whether it's words, a glance, a caress, an affirmation, or a note. Even a wink across the room is a way of staying in touch. With communication, you invite your partner to understand what it feels like to be you, and you make an effort to understand what it feels like to be them. So set a goal to maintain the beautiful, comforting feelings that come when the two of you are connected through give-and-take communication. Do a quick check as often as you can: "Did I show my partner that their thoughts and feelings matter to me?"

In marriage, you will be each other's best mirror. As you interact, you are a reflection of how you see the other. Be aware that what you reflect back through words and actions can either buoy their spirits or take the wind out of their sails. When you admire your partner, you hold the faith for them even when they are facing stress and can serve as a buffer against everyday challenges. Couples who set an intention to engage in supportive, healthy, and healing two-way communication are much more likely to have a long and happy life together.

WHAT TO SAY

Some couples who have spent much of their time on social media recognize the need to polish their art of conversation. Even those who haven't relied so much on technology find the need to learn how to communicate better. Here's how to involve yourselves in the kind of intimate conversation that will build the bond between you over the years ahead. Use the following discussions and prompts to reach deeper levels of sharing. When you've completed this "What to Say" section of the workbook, look over your responses and, as a couple, figure out which areas you have down pat and which you'd like to work on more.

1. Words of Affirmation

You can never go wrong by affirming what you love about your partner. In our busy times, positive feedback tends to be in short supply. Oftentimes, we can get so focused on something that's happening in the world that it dominates our thinking. Therefore, we need to consciously leave room for positive expression.

Any time you express your approval of something your partner has said or done, you are remembering and underlining the value of your relationship; this gives you a positive "snapshot" of your partner that you can cherish even when the world is distracting you. Develop the habit of noticing moments when you feel respect or admiration for your partner and share what you observe.

SHARE WORDS OF AFFIRMATION

What do you love about your partner? What words of positive affirmation can you offer? Take a moment to write down a few affirmations now and, after you've both had a chance to respond, discuss your responses.

❯ PARTNER A ❮

_____

_____

_____

❯ PARTNER B ❮

_____

_____

_____

Discussion Notes

_____

_____

_____

_____

2. Your Highs and Lows

Get into the habit of catching your partner up on the highs and lows of your day. Couples who do this stay in touch about what leads to excitement or disappointment, allowing them to cultivate the good things and mitigate the not-so-good things. You will also catch clues to better understand your partner's mood. Let your partner know you appreciate what they have shared and validate their experience by trying to see the situation from their perspective.

Take a moment now to reflect on your day. Share one thing with your partner that excited you and one thing that frustrated you in the space provided. You don't always need to write these things down, of course, but starting this way can help you get a feel for developing the habit.

>> PARTNER A <<

_____

_____

_____

>> PARTNER B <<

_____

_____

_____

Discussion Notes

_____

_____

_____

_____

3. What's Going on in Your Head

Your partner can't know what you're thinking if you don't tell them. Part of communicating is allowing your partner to know what's going on in your mind and not keeping it to yourself and giving it the chance to fester. Remaining silent on the thoughts that are weighing you down—whether or not they have to do with your relationship—doesn't do your partner (or you) any favors.

Take a moment now to share something in the space provided that's been on your mind that you haven't previously shared with your partner:

> PARTNER A <

_____

_____

_____

> PARTNER B <

_____

_____

_____

Discussion Notes

_____

_____

_____

_____

4. What Moves or Touches You

What moves or touches one person may be very different from what moves or touches another. One person might experience a flood of happy emotions when they witness an act of kindness. Another might feel moved when they hear a beautiful piece of music or when they watch their favorite sports team celebrating a victory. Sharing the everyday things as well as the big events that make you feel warm inside gives your partner a front-row seat into what makes you tick as a human being.

SHARE WHAT MAKES YOU TICK

Take a moment now to share with your partner what makes you feel warm and fuzzy inside. If it's something your partner does, by all means include that. I always ask the couples in my premarital sessions to recount a moment when their partner went the extra step to make them feel loved or cared for—when what they did *moved* them.

> **PARTNER A**

_____

_____

_____

> **PARTNER B**

_____

_____

_____

Discussion Notes

_____

_____

_____

_____

5. Your Interests and Observations

As a couple, you likely share interests and spend a lot of time together in various settings. This doesn't mean that you don't have your own interests and personal observations about the goings-on around you. For example, if you read an interesting article, share the highlights with your partner and why you found it interesting. If something funny happened at work, tell a story about it and why you found it funny. If you see a movie together, discuss what you each liked about it and what you didn't like.

TALK ABOUT WHAT INTERESTS YOU

Take a moment to think of something that interests you and share with your partner in the space provided what it is and why you are drawn to it:

> PARTNER A ‹

_____

_____

_____

> PARTNER B ‹

_____

_____

_____

_____

_____

_____

_____

_____

HOW TO SAY IT

You are probably familiar with the phrase, "It's not what you say; it's how you say it." For instance, you could say, "You look great," but it's the tone of your voice that can make this a compliment or a putdown. So, when you speak to your partner, make an effort to keep warmth and respect in your voice, especially if you need to discuss something that's uncomfortable. If you grew up in a family where respectful communication was in short supply, you may find yourself a bit limited in your vocabulary of compassionate sharing; you'll need to make an extra effort to develop your ability to communicate with compassion if you want to have a strong marriage.

When you are spending time together, approach your partner with an open heart, reminding yourself how much you appreciate having that person in your life. If you are harboring a grievance from a recent exchange, keep the biting comments and sarcastic tone at bay. If you really take in the person in front of you and gaze deeply into their eyes, your heart will open and your words will be expressed with the love, appreciation, and compassion you truly feel for them.

What if you know the conversation will be uncomfortable? Here are six steps for having this type of talk, whether it has to do with your relationship or another matter:

1. Keep your opening statements about the issue simple and straightforward with a neutral tone.
2. Cover the five Ws: who, what, when, where, and why. In other words, be sure to include all the factors involved in the situation without laying blame. (This works for sharing everyday stories, too.)

3. Explain how you are affected by the issue. In this way, you are sharing what it means to be you.
4. Explore what you want or hope to do about it without repeating steps 1 through 3.
5. Share an "I would love it if . . . " to ask your partner to do something that would work for you.
6. Ask for your partner's input. If the matter directly concerns your partner, work together to figure out an agreeable resolution.

EXPRESSING LOVE

Do you remember that first time you said, "I love you" to your partner? Recall how deeply devoted you felt to this person when you uttered those meaningful words. Couples who often tell each other "I love you" tend to hold on to the romance in their relationship, so make a pact now to develop an everyday habit out of expressing your love in words, even if it wasn't something you saw between your parents.

Saying "I love you" isn't the only way to express your love to your partner, of course. Learning early on what conveys a sense of love to your partner will give you a leg up on the best ways to express your affection. Don't be surprised to discover that you communicate in different languages of love. For example, if you say, *"Je t'aime,"* your partner (who does not speak French) will have no idea that you are saying "I love you." Similarly, different actions translate to love for different people. Therefore, you'll need to learn how to communicate in your partner's love language. If you haven't figured this out, just ask. Here are some examples of how your partner may show you that they love you (and vice versa):

1. Making you a special meal or bringing in your favorite foods.
2. Giving you a spontaneous gift or bouquet of flowers.
3. Listening to you with their full attention when you are sharing your thoughts.
4. Being supportive when you are making a choice or trying something new.
5. Taking care of little odds and ends that you can't get to.
6. Touching you or holding you in a pleasant, comforting way.
7. Expressing their approval or respect for you with words of affirmation.

8. Offering words of encouragement when you are struggling.
9. Going with you to your favorite destination or doing an activity with you that you love.
10. Wanting to spend time with you just hanging out.

Don't be surprised if you discover that you have been working awfully hard to express love in your language but not your partner's language. The following exercise will help you develop the skills to communicate your love in a way that you can both understand.

WHAT MAKES YOU FEEL LOVED

This worksheet includes a list of ways a person might express their love (there's room to add a few of your own if you don't see them here). If the particular action makes you feel loved, rank its impact on a scale from 1 (low) to 5 (high). If it doesn't make you feel loved, place an X in that row. (That doesn't mean you don't appreciate the effort, of course.) You'll have an opportunity to discuss the results with each other after you've both completed the exercise.

I FEEL LOVED WHEN YOU:	PARTNER A	PARTNER B
BRING ME FLOWERS		
DO ACTIVITIES WITH ME		
ENCOURAGE ME		
GIVE ME GIFTS		
GIVE ME YOUR FULL ATTENTION		
GO SHOPPING WITH ME		
GO TO SPORTING EVENTS WITH ME		
KISS ME		
MAKE ME A SPECIAL MEAL		
ORDER IN MY FAVORITE FOOD		

I FEEL LOVED WHEN YOU:	PARTNER A	PARTNER B
SAY "I LOVE YOU"		
SHARE YOUR THOUGHTS WITH ME		
SHOW ME APPROVAL AND/OR RESPECT		
SIT AND TALK WITH ME		
SNUGGLE WITH ME		
SUPPORT ME		
TAKE CARE OF LITTLE THINGS THAT NEED TO GET DONE		
TELL ME WHAT YOU LOVE ABOUT ME		
TOUCH ME		
WATCH MOVIES WITH ME		
WRITE ME LETTERS, EMAILS, AND/OR TEXTS		
ADD YOUR OWN	PARTNER A	PARTNER B

Partner Discussion

Are you surprised by your partner's love language? Did you know that some of the loving things you do can show your partner how deeply you care for them? Are there some things you'd like to start doing more of now that you know your partner experiences your love when you do them? Discuss the similarities and differences in how you show love and how you receive love. This is important information moving forward so that you both know how loved and important you are to each other.

Discussion Notes

DEALING WITH ANGER

Developing the habit of paying careful attention to each other's anger serves as an essential way to build a long-lasting bond. There's an art to dealing with your frustrations with each other, and when you master it, you will stand in good stead as you prepare to walk down the aisle and beyond.

Aristotle once said, "Anybody can become angry—that is easy, but to be angry with the right person and to the right degree and at the right time and for the right purpose, and in the right way—that is not within everybody's power and is not easy." This is an excellent observation. When you are feeling angry, think about Aristotle's statement. For instance, you may be angry with your partner over something that someone else did, you may blow it out of proportion, and your reason may be to make your partner feel bad because you feel bad. If you realize you are doing this, you can offer a sincere apology. Your partner can recognize that you've missed the mark and approach you with compassion rather than fueling the angry exchange.

Regardless of whether or not the anger was appropriate, you may find that each of you has a different attitude about anger, depending on the typical interactions you experienced growing up. Maybe you grew up in a family where any intense expression was frowned upon or any form of profanity would be considered inappropriate. Or if your family relished heated debates, you may expect your partner to be game, but it might not feel good to them. It's important to understand each other's learned style of expressing anger and frustration to avoid exacerbating the issue.

LEARNED STYLES OF DEALING WITH ANGER

What you witnessed growing up has given you one paradigm for dealing with frustration and anger. You may unconsciously slip into reenacting the script you learned from your parents as a child or you may have promised yourself never to respond to your partner the way your parents interacted. Getting this out on paper now can shed light on some of your habitual reactions and help you take steps to find better ways to deal with your anger. Complete these worksheets and then discuss.

QUESTIONS	NEVER	SELDOM	OFTEN
DID YOUR PARENTS DISPLAY ANY HOSTILITY TOWARD EACH OTHER IN FRONT OF YOU?			
DID YOUR PARENTS CALL EACH OTHER NAMES OR ATTACK EACH OTHER WITH PUTDOWNS?			
DID YOUR PARENTS GIVE EACH OTHER THE SILENT TREATMENT, LETTING THEIR ANGER SMOLDER?			
DID YOUR PARENTS' USE OF ALCOHOL MAKE THEIR ARGUMENTS WORSE?			
WHEN IT WAS DIRECTED AT YOU, DID YOUR PARENTS' ANGER SEEM APPROPRIATE?			
DO YOU THINK OUTSIDE PRESSURE MADE YOUR PARENTS TAKE THEIR ANGER OUT ON EACH OTHER, YOU, OR OTHER FAMILY MEMBERS?			
DID YOU FIGHT WITH YOUR SIBLINGS?			
WAS THERE ANY HITTING BETWEEN MEMBERS OF YOUR FAMILY DURING ARGUMENTS?			

> PARTNER B <

QUESTIONS	NEVER	SELDOM	OFTEN
DID YOUR PARENTS DISPLAY ANY HOSTILITY TOWARD EACH OTHER IN FRONT OF YOU?			
DID YOUR PARENTS CALL EACH OTHER NAMES OR ATTACK EACH OTHER WITH PUTDOWNS?			
DID YOUR PARENTS GIVE EACH OTHER THE SILENT TREATMENT, LETTING THEIR ANGER SMOLDER?			
DID YOUR PARENTS' USE OF ALCOHOL MAKE THEIR ARGUMENTS WORSE?			
WHEN IT WAS DIRECTED AT YOU, DID YOUR PARENTS' ANGER SEEM APPROPRIATE?			
DO YOU THINK OUTSIDE PRESSURE MADE YOUR PARENTS TAKE THEIR ANGER OUT ON EACH OTHER, YOU, OR OTHER FAMILY MEMBERS?			
DID YOU FIGHT WITH YOUR SIBLINGS?			
WAS THERE ANY HITTING BETWEEN MEMBERS OF YOUR FAMILY DURING ARGUMENTS?			

Partner Discussion

As you review these worksheets, approach each other with compassion. Share your stories, and talk about any implications. Do you see yourself slipping into a negative pattern based on your learned style of dealing with anger? If so, affirm your intentions to grow in that area and support each other's efforts.

Discussion Notes

_____

_____

_____

_____

_____

IDENTIFY YOUR HOT BUTTONS

A *hot button* is an issue that often gets blown out of proportion because it touched something in you that made you feel intense anger. Maybe your partner comments on an outfit you're wearing and doesn't mean to hurt your feelings, but the reaction you have stems from something that happened earlier in life, which you may or may not remember. You may have noticed that certain things your partner says upsets you but also that you are upset when other people say the same seemingly innocuous thing. You may also notice that you are more likely to overreact to a hot button when you are feeling tired, hungry, hurt, etc.

You may not be aware of what will set you off in the future, but you can certainly look over past interactions where you overreacted. You may have similar experiences in the days, months, and years to come, so this will likely be an ongoing investigation. For now, to shed some light on what might cause you to "see red," respond to the following prompts and be sure to include any extenuating circumstances that might have occurred prior to your blowup:

I remember overreacting when:

_____

_____

_____

_____

_____

I remember overreacting when:

_____

_____

_____

_____

_____

Partner Discussion

Discuss how you can work together to soothe each other when a hot button gets pressed. Complete this sentence: "When I'm triggered, I would love it if you would . . . "

Discussion Notes

_____

_____

_____

_____

_____

The next time either of you wants to bring up a concern or frustration with your partner, return to this workbook and take the following steps. You can also practice right now by taking turns:

1. Make sure you are feeling grounded and not overreactive.
2. Ask if it's a good time to talk; it may not be for your partner. If now is not a good time, ask for an alternate time.
3. Affirm the value of your relationship.
4. Describe the behavior you observed that bothered you.
5. Name what meaning you find yourself giving to what happened.
6. Share what you find yourself feeling as you see it that way.
7. Specifically name a yearning about the situation by saying, "I would love it if . . . "

If you identify the meaning you give to your partner's action, you can see how you arrived at your feeling. You no longer will find yourself saying, "You made me feel—." Instead, you will own that the meaning you gave to their action was the basis that led to your reaction. This will free you to attack less and ask for compassion and support around the things you want to change.

After you have taken these steps, add your individual observations about how the interaction went in the space provided.

> PARTNER A <

_____

_____

_____

_____

_____

_____

_____

_____

_____

_____

Partner Discussion

Discuss whether the partner on the receiving end of the frustration protocol responded with compassion rather than defensiveness. And discuss whether or not the partner using the protocol was able to avoid overacting. Agree to keep practicing until you can express frustration in a way that will help you build a bond that can sail through storms.

Discussion Notes

_____

_____

_____

_____

_____

PROCESS AND MODULATE YOUR ANGER

This exercise is intended to teach you how to process and quell your anger in a healthy way to avoid escalating arguments. For the purposes of this exercise, consider an old argument you may have had with your partner. Don't focus on any issues you may be facing currently until you've learned these steps. There's no need to write your answers down here, but you should each take some time to process the following steps.

1. Ask yourself, on a scale of 1 to 10, how angry you are. Giving the intensity of your feelings a number will prompt the rational side of your brain to kick in.

2. When your rational brain activates, identify the feelings that might be underlying your anger. Be honest with yourself about what those feelings are. Consider whether there are other factors outside of your feelings that might be increasing your anger, such as exhaustion, alcohol, stress, or anxiety.

3. Realize you have control over how you react to those feelings you've just identified, and that you are responsible for how your reaction to those feelings affects your relationship with your partner.

4. Ask yourself, "Do I want to be right or do I want to feel the bond with my partner?"

5. Knowing the above, ask yourself, "Is this level of anger valid in this situation? Or could this be considered an overreaction?" Be completely honest with yourself.

6. Consider whether there are other solutions to the issue that do not require anger.

Partner Discussion

The difficulty in this exercise is twofold: It asks you to be honest with yourself *about* yourself, and it asks you to allow your partner to do the same. We often find it much easier to point out others' flaws than to identify our own. When we act or speak in anger, it's often because we feel frustrated that the other person can't see where they are wrong and where we are right. The goal here is not to be "right"; it's to do right by each other. When anger arises, the argument is already lost for everyone. Discuss how you felt taking these steps. As you share your discoveries here, express gratitude for your partner's willingness to stick by you as you strive to approach disagreements in a healthy way to encourage growth and love in your future relationship.

Discussion Notes

_____

_____

_____

_____

_____

Making Different Styles Mesh

Many premarital couples face the challenge of having different styles of communicating anger and frustration based on what they learned from their families of origin. Naturally, it helps if you can steer away from assuming that what you find familiar is the right way to do things. Instead, discover what will work for *both* of you. When you are upset with each other, you may not be able to see each other's points of view. If you are really upset, you may feel like you can't rest until you get your partner to realize they are wrong.

This is why The Pause (see page 34) is so essential. By taking time-outs, you give yourselves a chance to discern the vulnerable feelings that may be beneath your anger. Reflecting on your disagreements with this in mind can lead to a better understanding of what the other needs. Here are some suggestions to help you make a difference:

1. Do you sometimes wish your partner would just listen until you finish? If so, ask for that. However, this will probably not work if your partner feels like they have a sense of where you are going with what you are saying. In that case, ask them if they can tell you what they suspect you are about to say. Listen to whether your partner was tracking where you were going. Respond with, "That's part of it, and here's what else I need to get on the table."

2. If your partner comes at you in an attacking way, ask them, "Could you say that differently? I really want to understand what you are saying." If that does not work, you may need to implement a pause.

THE PAUSE

You can learn to give each other a break when arguments start to escalate to avoid making the problem worse and then saying or doing things you might regret. When your body is saturated with emotions and adrenaline, it's called getting flooded. This is the perfect time to take a break. Here's how:

1. Agree ahead of time that either one of you can declare a unilateral cease-fire.

2. Notice the signs that you are becoming defensive and your anger is getting out of hand:

   - You have raised your voice.

   - You have quit listening to what your partner is saying.

   - You are interrupting with things like, "But you . . ."

   - You resort to attacking by saying things like, "Well you never loved me in the first place."

3. Acknowledge to yourself that your brain is about to be hijacked and turn to your partner and say:

   - "I am aware I am getting flooded." (Not, "You're making me feel flooded.")

   - "I am seeing things in black and white and may say things I don't want to say."

3. Respect when your partner needs to take a pause. Sometimes it may feel like your partner is ducking out of the argument. Agree to return to the concerns when you can both discuss the issue without being defensive.

Arguments happen. It's what you do with them and how you reconnect afterward that matters. Most clashes come from people seeing things differently. It may

- "I need some time to soothe myself."
- "I know this issue means a lot to you."
- "Could we pick up this conversation at the following appointed time when I would feel calmer?"
- "I love you." (This may be hard to say in the heat of the argument.)

4. Separate and challenge yourself to self-soothe by:
   - Taking a walk and drawing your attention away from the argument and observing nature.
   - Becoming absorbed in a book.
   - Taking a bath.
   - Listening to music that gives you a sense of peace.
   - Challenging yourself not to spend the time rehashing how wrong your partner is.

5. If you have asked for the pause and made an appointment, show up. Initiate the conversation, but always with, "Is this a good time?"

Rehearse asking for a time-out. You may feel amazed at how the words do not come trippingly off your tongue. You may need a few trial runs. Some couples report having tried this and thought it didn't work. It's usually because they have not followed through on steps 3, 4, and 5.

stem from divergent expectations, from yearnings that even you are unaware of, or from a deep sense of what people are supposed to do. Any one of these can cause you to view things from diverse angles.

Underneath conflicts often rests a desire to feel heard, to be respected, and to know that you can influence your partner to do something that matters to you. You need to address conflicts and not sweep them under the rug, which leads to smoldering and distancing.

DECISION-MAKING

As a couple, you have already been making decisions together—and one of the biggest was the decision to get married. You are on the same page with that! As a married couple, you will be making numerous decisions throughout the years, from where you will go on your honeymoon to where you will live and eventually retire. Learning to make win-win decisions will keep your relationship strong and steady. Here are five steps for making decisions that you will both be happy with:

1. Describe the nature of the decision that needs to be made.
2. Name the issues that will emerge if a good decision is not made (what are the problems you're trying to avoid or overcome?). Name the desired outcome that is likely to happen when a good decision is made (what experience do you want to have?).
3. Name all the ingredients of an ideal solution—in other words, how would you recognize a good plan if you came up with it?
4. Review the crazy and not-so-crazy choices and potential options and identify the one that meets the most criteria of your ideal solution.
5. Set up an action plan that includes the steps you'll take and when you will take them.

Following these steps will help you come back to each other and work out a solution that leaves your mutual admiration of each other intact. Being able to hold on to that underlying faith in your partner keeps your bond solid and secure.

PRACTICE THE DECISION-MAKING PROTOCOL

To practice your decision-making skills, identify a joint decision that each of you feels stuck on. For now, choose anything. The idea is to practice making small decisions so that you are more skilled at the process when larger decisions need to be made. Maybe for now, one of you will choose something like where to eat tonight for dinner and the other will choose what to give your friends as a wedding gift.

Decision to be made:

_____

Decision to be made:

_____

Partner Discussion

Flip a coin to decide which decision to make first. Follow the steps on page 36. Get playful with this. For example, if one of you choses what to eat for dinner tonight, the result of not making a good decision might be that the food didn't hit the spot or it was downright awful. When you're on step 4, one of your crazy options might be "Fly to Paris for a good meal at a bistro." That's not so crazy when you think about it because it might lead to you going out for tasty French food this evening. The idea here is to consider everything during the process and have fun together brainstorming what actions you will take to achieve a good outcome.

When you've completed the steps for each decision, talk about whether or not you both feel good about the decisions you have settled on. Also, discuss your experience of the process. Will you feel inclined to use the decision-making protocol often?

Discussion Notes

_____

_____

_____

_____

_____

DISCUSSING ISSUES OF PRIVACY

Now's the time to develop some ground rules around privacy. Discussions now can help you avoid surprises in the future. On the one hand, you may share everything on Facebook with everybody. Or you may prefer a high level of control over what your partner tells the world on social media. Both of you could possibly slip into a strong sense of what's right or wrong based on what's been the norm for you with your family or friends.

In the middle of fights in which neither of you is processing shades of gray, your clarity about what the other "should not do" may become emphatic. Naming what you believe to be a boundary crossing into your privacy will head off some battles at the pass. A simple example is discovering that you feel it's an invasion of your privacy for your partner to use your razor or other toiletry items. Here are some examples of what someone might consider a significant boundary crossing:

1. Reading the other's diary or journal.
2. Listening in on phone conversations when your partner is unaware that you are overhearing.
3. Reading your partner's text messages or emails unless you are both comfortable with that.
4. Talking about your feelings about your partner with people if your partner objects.

As a couple, you need to map out what feels right to the other and what feels safe. As circumstances continue to change, you will need to review your ground rules. This becomes complicated if you've done something that raises issues of trust, such as getting too close to someone else. Many partners will say to me, "I know I should never have read their email but I wondered what was going on." The better part of valor is first to share your suspicion and ask.

NAME YOUR BOUNDARIES

This exercise will help you clearly identify your own boundaries and clearly understand your partner's boundaries. After you've each answered the following prompts, you will have the opportunity to discuss your answers.

I would appreciate it if you would never:

_____

_____

Please ask my permission before you:

_____

_____

I would consider it a breach of my privacy if you:

_____

_____

_____

> PARTNER B <

I would appreciate it if you would never:

_____

_____

Please ask my permission before you:

_____

_____

I would consider it a breach of my privacy if you:

_____

_____

Partner Discussion

Discussing boundaries may raise feelings of defensiveness. Your partner's willingness to discuss their boundaries with you is a sign of trust. They're trusting you to acknowledge their boundaries without taking them personally or trying to renegotiate them, and they're trusting you to respect those boundaries. Do your best to be worthy of that trust and to show the same trust in them.

_____

_____

_____

_____

_____

COUPLE CHECK-IN

Flip back through this chapter and review your responses to the exercises. Were there any sticking points that one or both of you would like to revisit and work on more? What were your three biggest takeaways from this part of the workbook? Take notes in the spaces provided and discuss the items you've listed. Make an agreement to return to the exercises you would like to work further on before moving ahead to the next chapter.

> PARTNER A

Exercises I would like to work on more:

_____

_____

_____

_____

_____

My three biggest takeaways were:

1. _____

2. _____

3. _____

Exercises I would like to work on more:

_____

_____

_____

_____

_____

My three biggest takeaways were:

1. _____

2. _____

3. _____

ACTION STEPS

1. Hide a note that your partner will find expressing your gratitude for something they did that made you feel loved.
2. Have a debate about a political issue you might disagree on to see if you can find ways to hear the other without becoming angry or frustrated.
3. Pick a decision that you both want to make around something fun, to see if you can come up with an idea using the decision-making steps on page 36.
4. Identify a potential conflict having to do with your wedding. Try to view the situation from your partner's perspective and see if you can arrive at a solution before the conflict even arises by using effective communication skills.
5. Pay attention to how your friends and family communicate. Incorporate what you admire about their styles into your interactions with each other and identify styles you want to avoid.

CHAPTER

3

Money

FOR SOME COUPLES, FINANCES can become one of the hot-button issues we discussed in chapter 2 because financial matters often involve one's feelings of safety, security, and status. By getting married, you are essentially creating a financial institution. Over the years, you will hopefully build your financial reserves and create a solid foundation for your retirement. Addressing your financial styles and goals is a critical part of premarital counseling to make sure you wind up with a method for spending and saving that works for both of you. This chapter will help you develop habits that will help you feel like competent managers of your funds.

YOUR FINANCIAL SITUATION

It might sound extreme, but some people would rather stand on a street corner naked than reveal the truth about their finances. That's okay in most cases; the amount of money we have is really nobody else's business—that is, until it comes to our partners.

It is essential to clarify now what each of you has available in the way of monetary resources, as well as any debts you owe, in order to provide the groundwork for a trusting relationship around your finances. Working together to deal with the reality of your finances strengthens your bond and helps you work toward your financial goals for building your future together. Keeping bad news about your finances to yourself until after you are married creates distrust. Avoid it.

DISCLOSE YOUR FINANCIAL STATUS

In the worksheet below, record the amount of money you currently have available and how much money you owe to give each other an accurate picture of your monetary situation. Be aware that many couples begin their married life together with some debt on both sides. Now is the time to bring it out into the open. Although one or both of you may feel some shame about what you owe, keep in mind that the best antidote for shame is sharing. When partners accept each other's reality, they can start a plan to build from there; it's a model for acceptance.

ASSETS	CHECKING ACCOUNT(S)	SAVINGS ACCOUNT(S)	INVESTMENT ACCOUNT(S)	PROPERTY VALUE	INHERITANCE	OTHER
PARTNER A						
PARTNER B						

DEBTS	CAR LOAN	STUDENT LOAN	PARENT LOAN	MORTGAGE	ALIMONY OR CHILD SUPPORT	CREDIT CARDS
PARTNER A						
PARTNER B						

Partner Discussion

As you take a look at the reality of your financial resources and debts, allow yourselves to acknowledge the truth of where you are. Discuss any feelings you have about having disclosed this information and about seeing the other's financial picture.

Discussion Notes

_____

_____

_____

_____

_____

SPENDING VERSUS SAVING

Here's another area where you may begin to notice differences in how you operate. One partner may make money to spend it, and the other partner may feel steeped in the value of saving carefully to build for a secure future. You may also both be spenders or savers or somewhere in between. The following exercises will dig really deep to help you closely examine why each of you approaches spending and saving the way you do. This information will be invaluable in your efforts to figure out what works for both of you as a married couple.

WORD ASSOCIATIONS

List all of the words or phrases that come to mind when you think of the word money. Some examples might be, "Never enough" or "Whoopee, let's spend it!" or "I am afraid to spend even a penny" or "Security" or "Food" or "Time" or maybe even "The root of all evil." Get creative here and write as many words and phrases as you can to get it all out into the open. Approach this exercise playfully!

> PARTNER A <

_____

_____

_____

_____

_____

_____

_____

_____

_____

_____

Partner Discussion

Did you laugh at your discoveries? I hope so. Sometimes when we free associate, we come up with all sorts of wacky responses. Still, there's probably a lot of truth here. See if you can determine how these thoughts have shaped how you each deal with finances. Discuss how you can work around any negative associations so you can grow beyond them.

Discussion Notes

_____

_____

_____

_____

_____

LEARNED STYLES OF HANDLING MONEY

This worksheet includes a list of ways your parents might have handled their finances. Each partner will have an opportunity to identify whether or not a particular statement is true in their case. If so, rank how true it was on a scale from 1 (low) to 5 (high). If it doesn't apply, place an X in that row. You'll have an opportunity to discuss the results with each other after you've both completed the exercise.

STATEMENT	PARTNER A	PARTNER B
ONE OR BOTH OF MY PARENTS LIKED TO SPEND MONEY.		
MY PARENTS SAVED FOR THEIR RETIREMENT.		
MY PARENTS HAD A GOOD SYSTEM FOR HOW THEY SHARED THEIR MONEY AND HOW THEY PAID THE BILLS.		
MY PARENTS BUDGETED THEIR MONEY WELL.		
MONEY WAS A CONSTANT SOURCE OF STRESS FOR MY PARENTS.		
MY PARENTS FOUGHT OFTEN ABOUT MONEY.		
MY PARENTS NEVER MENTIONED MONEY IN FRONT OF ME.		
ONLY ONE OF MY PARENTS HANDLED THE FINANCES.		
MY PARENTS CAUTIONED ME ABOUT SPENDING MONEY.		
MY PARENTS MADE ME SPEND MY OWN MONEY ON SPECIAL ITEMS.		
MY PARENTS OFTEN BOUGHT ME WHAT I ASKED FOR.		

Partner Discussion

What did you discover about how each set of your parents handled matters concerning money that might influence your approach as a married couple? Ask deep questions of each other about what it was like to hear your parents discussing their finances or to have no firm idea where your family stood when it came to finances.

Discussion Notes

_____

_____

_____

_____

_____

This worksheet includes a list of possible personal experiences you had in your family concerning money. As with earlier exercises, each partner will have an opportunity to identify whether or not a particular statement is true in their case. If so, rank how true it was on a scale from 1 (low) to 5 (high). If it doesn't apply, place an X in that row. You'll have an opportunity to discuss the results with each other after you've both completed the exercise.

STATEMENT	PARTNER A	PARTNER B
WE HAD ADEQUATE HOUSING.		
WE HAD PLENTY TO EAT.		
WE WERE OFTEN IN DEBT.		
WE WERE NOT PERMITTED LUXURIES.		
WE OFTEN DISCUSSED MONEY.		
WE HAD AN EXTRAVAGANT LIFESTYLE.		
MY FAMILY INHERITED THEIR WEALTH.		
MY FAMILY FRETTED OVER MONEY.		
MY FAMILY FILED FOR BANKRUPTCY.		

Partner Discussion

Did you discover things about your partner's past that you didn't already know? You are each starting to get a fuller picture of what it was like to grow up in a family that may have been different from your own when it came to financial matters. Discuss the similarities and differences. Based on your answers in the previous exercises, share with each other how you would like to handle financial matters in your own home.

Discussion Notes

_____

_____

_____

_____

FINANCIAL PREFERENCES AND PRIORITIES

Now that you have discussed your different family and personal experiences about money, let's get more specific for each of you with your own preferences and priorities around finances. As before, each partner will have an opportunity to identify whether or not a particular statement is true in their case. If so, rank how true it is on a scale from 1 (low) to 5 (high). If it doesn't apply, place an X in that row. You'll have an opportunity to discuss the results with each other after you've both completed the exercise.

I WOULD PREFER IT IF:	PARTNER A	PARTNER B
WE CREATE A WEEKLY OR MONTHLY BUDGET AND STICK TO IT.		
WE PAY OFF OUR CREDIT CARD BILLS EACH MONTH TO AVOID PAYING INTEREST.		
WE BUY ONLY WHAT WE HAVE SAVED MONEY FOR.		
WE DISCUSS ANY LARGE PURCHASES BEFORE WE MAKE THEM.		
WE PUT A PORTION OF OUR EARNINGS INTO OUR SAVINGS ACCOUNT WITH EACH PAYCHECK.		
WE ALLOW THE IRS TO WITHHOLD THE MAXIMUM AMOUNT FROM OUR PAYCHECKS SO THAT WE GET A SIZABLE RETURN LATER ON TO SPEND ON SOMETHING WE WANT.		
WE START PUTTING MONEY TOWARD OUR FUTURE CHILDREN'S COLLEGE FUND RIGHT AWAY.		

I WOULD PREFER IT IF:	PARTNER A	PARTNER B
WE INVEST IN A HOUSE AS SOON AS WE CAN SO THAT IT INCREASES IN VALUE FOR POSSIBLE RESALE TO BUY A LARGER HOUSE WHEN WE NEED IT.		
WE BOTH CONTRIBUTE TO A RETIREMENT FUND SO WE CAN FEEL SECURE ABOUT THE FUTURE.		
WE EACH HAVE A DISCRETIONARY BUDGET TO SPEND ON OUR HOBBIES AND INTERESTS.		
ADD YOUR OWN	PARTNER A	PARTNER B

Partner Discussion

Now you're getting a more complete picture of where you line up and where you differ. This is good fodder for putting your decision-making skills into practice. In areas where you don't see eye to eye, figure out a way to meet in the middle by compromising and come up with some win-win solutions.

Discussion Notes

_____

_____

_____

_____

_____

IDENTIFY YOUR FINANCIAL STYLES

What is your financial style? What is your partner's financial style? Once again, each partner will have an opportunity to identify whether or not a particular statement is true in their case with regard to your personal financial styles. Rank how true it is on a scale from 1 (low) to 5 (high). If it doesn't apply, place an X in that row. You'll have an opportunity to discuss the results with each other after you've both completed the exercise.

STATEMENT	PARTNER A	PARTNER B
I KEEP DETAILED RECORDS OF INCOMING AND OUTGOING FUNDS.		
I AM ALWAYS MINDFUL OF HOW MUCH MONEY I AM SPENDING.		
IT IS IMPORTANT TO ME TO SAVE UP MONEY FOR FUN ACTIVITIES AND VACATIONS.		
I WANT TO INVEST IN A HOUSE.		
I WOULD LIKE TO HAVE MONEY TO PASS ON TO OUR FUTURE CHILDREN.		
I WANT TO HAVE A VERY SOLID RETIREMENT PLAN.		
I DON'T BALANCE MY CHECKBOOK.		
I WANT TO GIVE MONEY TO CHARITY.		
I TEND TO BE MISERLY WITH MONEY.		
I SOMETIMES SPEND MORE MONEY THAN I HAVE AVAILABLE.		
I LIVE ON CREDIT.		
ADD YOUR OWN	PARTNER A	PARTNER B

Partner Discussion

Congratulate each other for your honesty. Some of these things might be difficult to admit, but as a married couple, you will want to know where each of you stands with regard to your financial future. As always, try to meet in the middle and help each other out with tasks and approaches that might be more difficult for one of you. For instance, is one of you great at math? That person can balance the checkbook each month. The other might be a good planner. That person can figure out when the bills need to get paid. How will you divide up financial tasks?

_____

_____

_____

_____

_____

BANK ACCOUNTS: JOINT, SEPARATE, OR BOTH?

Very soon, you will need to plan for how you will handle your banking. That includes who pays for what, who writes the checks or sets up the autopayments, and who watches the bottom line. Will you pool your money, keep it separate, or keep some of it separate?

There are three main benefits of having a shared account: 1) You can each withdraw cash as needed, 2) you can access the account online to see the balance and what withdrawals have been made by your partner, and 3) you can use it to pay basic household expenses and other couple-type expenses that keep your everyday life running.

If you decide to have a shared account, you'll also need to decide how to fund it. Will your individual salaries be deposited into this account, or will you fund it from your separate accounts? Either way, you may want your employer to make direct deposits into the account so you can cross one more thing off your to-do list. Automatic withdrawals for recurring bills, such as your mortgage or rent payment, can be helpful as well for making sure your bills get paid on time.

What reason might you and your partner have for wanting separate personal accounts? Perhaps one of you has inherited money that you want to keep separate. Or maybe you want to have a personal account to withdraw from for gifts and personal luxuries. If one of you has debt, such as a student loan, you may want to be in charge of paying it off from your own funds. Or maybe one of you feels that you are better at saving for a rainy day and want that security of knowing the money will be there when you need it.

Some couples have at least three accounts (one joint and two personal) and agree on how much money each should contribute to the joint account for the household expenses. Sometimes this might be based on a fair contribution that considers your individual incomes. Some couples use a percentage of each salary that seems equitable to fund their joint account.

DECIDE HOW TO SET UP YOUR ACCOUNTS

Discuss how you want to set up your accounts. What do you both feel will work best for you with regard to pooling your funds and/or keeping some funds separate? Here are some options. Together, check what you both think will work for you as a married couple, keeping in mind that as your circumstances change, you may want to revisit your plan:

- ☐ We will have a joint checking account and a joint savings account. All of our money will be pooled together.
- ☐ We will have a joint checking account and joint savings account, but we will also have our own separate accounts.
- ☐ We will have a joint checking account but separate savings accounts.
- ☐ We will have a joint checking account and separate checking accounts. We will each contribute to the joint account with an agreed-upon amount.
- ☐ We will each have our own checking account and savings account and be responsible for paying a fair share of the household expenses.
- ☐ Other: _____
- ☐ Other: _____

PAYING BILLS AND OTHER EXPENSES

If you and your partner have joined your finances into one account, to whatever extent, you'll need to decide who will be responsible for making sure the bills are paid from that account. One of you may seem like the obvious choice. That said, the designated bill payer may not exactly love the job, so the other will need to remember to express gratitude for their doing so and may need to make concessions by taking on other responsibilities for the household.

If you have separate accounts, you'll need to discuss how you will split costs between those accounts. There are many ways to do this, so find the one that works for both of you. Once you've divided your expenses, establish a time every week or month, depending on your billing schedule, for you both to sit down and discuss what bills have been paid and what bills are upcoming. Be willing to ask for and give help when it's needed. This will help you avoid "nagging" your partner and will reassure each of you that all the bills have been taken care of.

Recognize the importance of voicing your needs and concerns to your partner. Have an open, compassionate discussion and try to hear your partner's concerns. If old feelings from your past arise, discuss them without accusation. The goal is to establish a healthy financial relationship with your partner.

WHO PAYS FOR THE WEDDING?

Engaged couples sometimes have an issue determining how they will pay for the wedding. In some cases, they fall back on the tradition in which the bride's parents pay for the wedding and the groom's parents pay for the rehearsal dinner (if both sets of parents have the money to fund these sometimes extravagant events). There's no rule that says these traditions must be followed. Maybe each set of parents will contribute to the events, or maybe they can't or won't help out at all.

You will need to figure out what the two of you can afford when planning your wedding. If you feel comfortable, you can ask your parents if they will contribute, or they may have already told you that they would give you money toward the event or finance it in total. Parents often like to invite friends and extended family to their children's wedding and may agree to pay for the number of people they want to invite. Sometimes older relatives like grandparents and aunts and uncles may give you a sizable gift toward your wedding and/or honeymoon. None of this can be taken for granted. You probably have a good idea of what your parents and relatives are willing to do. If not, ask if it seems appropriate.

Chances are you have already budgeted for or planned your wedding. If not, now is a good time to start considering what's involved and how much you will spend on each item and who will be responsible for paying for or contributing to each aspect of the event. Work together to complete this worksheet.

EXPENSE	COST	CONTRIBUTOR
INVITATIONS		
WEDDING ATTIRE		
RINGS		
CEREMONY		
PHOTOGRAPHY		
RECEPTION VENUE		
FLOWERS AND DECORATIONS		
FOOD AND DRINK		
MUSIC		
TRANSPORTATION		
OTHER:		
OTHER:		

BUDGETING

To some, creating a budget sounds like an insurmountable task; to others, it can seem as natural as brushing their teeth. Maybe one or both of you are good with numbers, or maybe you both struggle in this area. A simple first step is to identify the amount of your net income (the amount you receive after taxes and any contributions) as well as any other income you regularly receive. Then, detail your monthly expenses. In the worksheet to follow, common expenses are listed in alphabetical order. Start with this worksheet but make a plan to create your own spreadsheet that lists your expenses in order of importance or amount.

FINDING A FINANCIAL ADVISOR

You may find it prudent to hire a financial advisor who can help you get off to the right financial start. Sharing your similarities and differences with a trained professional can help you develop a financial strategy that will work for both of you with a little compromise.

A financial advisor can help you identify ways to save on taxes and plan your investment strategy. They can also help you develop a budget as you work toward your goals and provide you with future projections based on your income and expenses. A good financial advisor can even lend you a hand as you deal with emotional issues surrounding money and help you normalize them.

Be on the alert for any financial planners who sell only their products. Make sure that whomever you hire advises you on a portfolio that does not include investments just from their shop. Here are some tips to find the right financial advisor for you:

1. Make sure that they are a certified financial planner (CFP). This means that they are not only licensed and regulated but also take mandatory classes to keep up on all aspects of financial matters as well as ethics classes.

2. Differentiate between those who charge a flat fee or charge based on commission. If you pay a flat fee, it might be a set amount for a financial plan or it might be a percentage of what you have invested. If you are using a commission-based advisor, they will be compensated for all transactions and may steer you in a particular direction that helps them as well.

3. Make sure you choose someone who has in their code of ethics the word fiduciary, which ensures that your advisor will help you make decisions that are in your best interest, not something that is just suitable for you.

4. Talk to friends and relatives for a suggestion. Someone in a financial situation similar to yours will probably know a planner who works with your level of assets.

5. Find someone with whom you both feel comfortable and seems to have time to answer whatever questions you have.

MONTHLY INCOME	PARTNER A	PARTNER B
SALARY		
OTHER:		
OTHER:		
OTHER:		
TOTAL:		

MONTHLY EXPENSES	PARTNER A	PARTNER B	SHARED EXPENSE
ALIMONY OR CHILD SUPPORT			
BANKING FEES			
CAR INSURANCE			
CAR PAYMENT			
CAR REPAIRS			
CELL PHONE			
CHARITABLE DONATIONS			
CHILDCARE/BABYSITTER/NANNY			
CLOTHING			
DINING OUT			
ELECTRICITY AND GAS/OIL			
GASOLINE			
GROCERIES			
HEALTH INSURANCE			
HEALTHCARE PRACTITIONERS			
HOMEOWNER'S INSURANCE			
LAUNDRY			
LOANS			
MORTGAGE OR RENT			
PARKING AND TOLLS			
PET CARE			
PRESCRIPTION MEDICATIONS			
PROPERTY TAXES			
TRANSPORTATION			

MONTHLY EXPENSES	PARTNER A	PARTNER B	SHARED EXPENSE
TUITION			
OTHER:			
OTHER:			
OTHER:			
OTHER:			
TOTALS:			

Adapted from **https://www.consumer.gov/sites/www.consumer.gov/files/pdf-1020 -make-budget-worksheet_form.pdf.**

Partner Discussion

Filling out this information for the first time may feel a little overwhelming. Take a deep breath and explore together how you can make your budget work. How does your income compare to your expenses? Are you able to cover your expenses or might you be setting yourselves up to live beyond your means? If you are, think about areas where you can cut back or make some changes.

Discussion Notes

_____

_____

_____

_____

_____

FIND WAYS TO SAVE MONEY

As a couple, review the following list and, if needed, check off the items you agree to in order to cut back on some of your expenses. There are blank lines to add some of your own ideas, so brainstorm other ways you can cut back and support each other in sticking to your plan.

- [ ] Shop around for less expensive auto insurance and home-owner's insurance.
- [ ] Negotiate with your cellular service to get your fees reduced or combine plans to save on the second phone.
- [ ] Eliminate your landline if you already have cell phones.
- [ ] Cancel monthly subscriptions to apps and services you don't use frequently.
- [ ] Speak to your cable company to see if they can offer you a lower rate.
- [ ] Clip coupons for restaurants and items you normally purchase at full price.
- [ ] Order takeout rather than eat at a restaurant to save on beverages and the tip.
- [ ] Invite friends over for dinner rather than meet at a restaurant.
- [ ] Cook your own meals whenever possible.
- [ ] Bring a bagged lunch to work.
- [ ] Unplug all electronic devices that are not in use.
- [ ] Watch movies on cable rather than go to a theater or cancel cable and treat yourself to a movie at a theater once a month.
- [ ] Go to the library for books you'd like to read rather than buy them.
- [ ] Make sure the tires on your cars are properly inflated to save on gas.
- [ ] Plan staycations rather than vacations.
- [ ] Make a grocery shopping list and purchase only what is on the list.
- [ ] Other: _____
- [ ] Other: _____
- [ ] Other: _____
- [ ] Other: _____
- [ ] Other: _____

PLAN TO PAY OFF DEBT

Earlier you disclosed any debt you have to your partner. That's a great start, but no matter the amount, you can't just shut your eyes and make it disappear. Instead, you will want to come together as a couple and use prudent judgment about how best to deal with it and know that you are wise to start bringing it down. Whatever debt you bring to the present, treat it like a philosopher: *It is what it is.* Making a plan to pay it off is your saving grace.

Once again, record your debt here; this time include any accrued interest and interest that will accrue in the near future:

DEBT	CAR LOAN	STUDENT LOAN	PARENT LOAN	MORTGAGE	ALIMONY OR CHILD SUPPORT	CREDIT CARDS
PARTNER A						
PARTNER B						
TOTAL						

Looking at the budget you created earlier, determine how much money you can apply toward your debt each month. Can you consolidate any credit cards and get a low-interest or no-interest account for a certain period? Are there any smaller amounts you can pay right away? Paying a smaller amount and crossing that debt off your list can be a psychological boost. However, a prudent way to approach what you owe is to pay off the accounts with the highest interest rate first to keep your debt from growing.

As a couple, use your decision-making skills to decide which debts you will tackle first. List the debt and the amount you will put toward it each month and about how long it will take to pay it off:

DEBT	MONTHLY AMOUNT	NUMBER OF MONTHS

DEBT	MONTHLY AMOUNT	NUMBER OF MONTHS

CREATE LONG-TERM FINANCIAL GOALS

At this stage of your engagement, you may not have focused on your long-term financial goals, wanting instead to make sure you can pay for your wedding and honeymoon. Yet now is the time to begin the conversation about your long-term goals. This worksheet includes a number of future-oriented desires and space to fill in any of your own. Each partner will have an opportunity to identify whether or not a particular statement is true in their case. If so, rank how true it is on a scale from 1 (low) to 5 (high). If it doesn't apply, place an X in that row. You'll have an opportunity to discuss the results with each other after you've both completed the exercise.

FINANCIAL GOALS	PARTNER A	PARTNER B
I WANT TO PAY OFF ANY DEBT AS SOON AS POSSIBLE.		
I WANT TO CREATE AN EMERGENCY FUND (OF THREE TO SIX MONTHS' SALARY) IN CASE OF A JOB LOSS OR AN UNEXPECTED EXPENSE THAT BLOWS THE BUDGET.		
I WANT TO PARTICIPATE IN MY COMPANY'S RETIREMENT PLAN.		
I WANT TO PLAN FOR THE COMPLETION OF COLLEGE OR GRADUATE SCHOOL.		
I WANT TO SAVE FOR SIGNIFICANT EXPENDITURES SUCH AS A NEW HOME, NEW CAR, OR HOME IMPROVEMENTS.		
I WANT TO BUY ENOUGH INSURANCE TO PAY FOR CONTINGENCIES.		
I WANT TO MAKE INVESTMENTS WITH THE HELP OF OUR FINANCIAL ADVISOR.		
I WANT TO SAVE FOR FUTURE VACATIONS.		
I WANT TO SAVE FOR A VACATION HOME IN A DESTINATION WE LOVE.		
I WANT TO BE ABLE TO LEAVE AN INHERITANCE FOR OUR FAMILY.		

ADD YOUR OWN	PARTNER A	PARTNER B

Partner Discussion

Once again, discuss as a couple where your ideas for your financial future line up and where they differ. Talk about why something is or isn't important to one or both of you. You might not be in a financial position to make much of this happen right now, but remember, you are just starting out, and when you work together to brainstorm ways to create the future you want to have, you will see your money tree grow with effort, good planning, and discipline.

Discussion Notes

_____

_____

_____

_____

_____

COUPLE CHECK-IN

Flip back through this chapter and review your responses to the exercises. Were there any sticking points that one or both of you would like to revisit and work on more? What were your three biggest takeaways from this part of the workbook? Take notes in the spaces provided and discuss the items you've listed. Make an agreement to return to the exercises you would like to work further on before moving ahead to the next chapter.

Exercises I would like to work on more:

_____

_____

_____

_____

_____

_____

My three biggest takeaways were:

1. _____

2. _____

3. _____

Exercises I would like to work on more:

_____

_____

_____

_____

_____

_____

My three biggest takeaways were:

1. _____

2. _____

3. _____

ACTION ITEMS

1. Now that you've laid all your cards on the table, plan a celebration. If it's within your budget, go out for a nice dinner. If not, take a homemade picnic to a nearby park. During this meal, share your appreciation of each other's honesty and efforts to get on the same financial page.

2. Ask close mutual friends about their financial goals and how they plan to save for them. This isn't about sharing specifics about one's financial status but rather bouncing ideas off each other to see what works when it comes to spending and saving.

3. Speak with an older couple who seems financially stable. Ask them what they have learned over the years when it came to conflicts around money.

4. Choose a charity that you both want to support and make your first joint donation.

5. Make a game of reporting back to each other how you saved money that day. For example, did you use a travel mug for your homemade coffee instead of buying an overpriced coffee on your way to work?

CHAPTER

4

Intimacy

WHEN WE TALK ABOUT intimacy, we are describing a strong emotional connection. As you move deeper into your relationship, you are beginning to plumb the depths of what this means. In getting close to your partner, you will catch glimpses of yourself that you have never known. At the same time, you will discover infinitely fascinating facets of the person you want to spend your life with. You may even begin to intuit what the other is thinking. You have a feeling that strong forces could not break your bond. Here you will find out how to protect the bond between you and how to keep it stable and thriving for a lifetime.

Communication, as you've learned, serves as the lifeblood of your relationship. Talking with your partner when you are relaxed and your guards are down will boost your sense of closeness and togetherness. In this chapter, you will learn what matters most in intimacy. You will have a chance to practice the habits that will enhance your dialogue and make your intimate connection last.

EXPRESSING AFFECTION

If you are an animal lover, you probably delight over being greeted by a happy dog with a wagging tail. Wouldn't it be nice if we all greeted each other that way? Not to confuse a person with a dog, of course, but that level of excitement and affection is such a feel-good experience that we can take a lesson from our canine companions.

Don't hesitate to greet your partner with exuberance and a warm embrace. Make it a habit to hug each other every day when you first see each other and after being apart. Feeling your partner's enthusiasm to welcome you into their presence is a joyful experience. Pause a moment to take it in and treat it as the precious act that it is. Some couples even remind themselves that if a tragedy were to happen, this could be the last time they see each other. While that might be a little intense, at least let your love be known at each and every encounter.

GAZE INTO EACH OTHER'S EYES

Eyes are the windows to the soul. Significant eye contact will deepen your intense feelings for each other. Build the habit of taking time to give your partner your full attention by making eye contact and catch the emotions that move between you. Here's an exercise to give each other your full attention right now in a deeply meaningful way:

1. Find a comfortable position where you can sit across from each other.
2. Set a timer for two minutes.
3. Gaze into each other's eyes. It's okay to blink but don't look away.
4. Relax into being with each other while gazing into each other's eyes.
5. When the timer goes off, you can break your gaze. You have my permission to continue longer if you'd like, as long as you both feel comfortable.

Partner Discussion

How did it feel to gaze into each other's eyes for two minutes or more? Discuss the emotions that came up for you. Did you giggle or laugh? Did you tear up? Did you feel awkward, uncomfortable, or self-conscious? Did you feel more intimate? What thoughts crossed your mind? Freely discuss the experience. There are no right or wrong answers.

Discussion Notes

_____

_____

_____

_____

_____

FEEDBACK ON EXCHANGES OF AFFECTION

Think back over the past week or month about your partner's overtures of affection. Mark where you would place their efforts on the continuum.

PARTNER A

A Little Distant   Just Right   A Little Overdone

●   ●   ●   ●   ●   ●   ●   ●   ●   ●

PARTNER B

A Little Distant   Just Right   A Little Overdone

●   ●   ●   ●   ●   ●   ●   ●   ●   ●

As you review your response to this exercise, use examples to describe particular moments and what worked or didn't work for you. If your responses fell to the left or right of the continuum, approach the topic with compassion and explain what you would like more or less of.

Discussion Notes

_____

_____

_____

_____

FORMS OF INTIMACY

Sometimes when we think of intimacy, we may not consider all of its variations, so let's review the three specific forms. This workbook is intended to help you establish lasting practices that will strengthen your lifelong bond. When being intimate, be sure to include each of these in your repertoire.

1. **Intellectual intimacy** occurs when you talk about issues and dialogue to make sense of things. In those moments, you feel excited about learning from each other. You may share a book or an article that the two of you can discuss to come up with its meaning for your lives.
2. **Emotional intimacy** develops when you share feelings about what's going on in your life. Some couples make their meals emotionally intimate by turning off all screens, notifications, and rings and catching up on all that matters. Taking time to share what it is like to be you with your partner and vice versa will keep you connected.
3. **Physical intimacy** tops many couples' lists. Some partners find an infinite amount of pleasure in caressing, holding each other, and spooning. Of course, sexual intimacy offers couples the most profound

kind of bonding experience and becomes a great stress reliever. For many couples, this leads to that wonderful feeling of "all's right with the world."

Intimacy of all kinds becomes the beautiful tie that gives you a sense of "we." Those conversations, those touches, that smile, a kiss or a hug—all of these remind you that someone has been waiting for you and you have been looking forward to seeing them. In essence, you have come home.

RELIVE MOMENTS OF INTIMACY

Take time now to recall various intimate moments you've shared as a couple for each form of intimacy. These are times when you felt especially close and connected. Jot them down below and then share them with each other. You can start with the phrase: *The time when we . . .*

PARTNER A

Moment of Intellectual Intimacy

_____

Moment of Emotional Intimacy

_____

Moment of Sexual Intimacy

_____

PARTNER B

Moment of Intellectual Intimacy

_____

Moment of Emotional Intimacy

_____

Moment of Sexual Intimacy

_____

Partner Discussion

Explore your experiences as if you are reviewing snapshots of your intimate moments. Feel the sense of warmth in your body as you discuss these experiences. How does it make you feel? Use these feelings as a barometer for your intimacy level. If you start to drift and lose touch a bit, you will be more likely to recognize the disconnect by knowing how you feel when you are connected. By staying aware, you can tap into the feelings to keep your relationship thriving.

Discussion Notes

_____

_____

_____

_____

_____

ABSENCE AND THE HEART

Absence *can* make the heart grow fonder, but you still need to stay connected. It is likely there will be times when one of you needs to travel for work or to visit family. Some partners relish the alone time and catch up on independent activities. Just be mindful to check in with each other while you are apart to maintain the solidness of your connection. Staying in contact while one of you is away can be challenging if you are in different time zones or if a business trip is particularly demanding.

It's often the case that when one partner is missing the other and there's little or no communication, that partner may slip into a mistaken sense that the other person just isn't there for them. It is more likely that their partner is just busy or so caught up in a new scenario that checking in is not on the top of their mind. Try not to wait too long before checking in.

Bend over backward to ensure that each of you feels connected by staying in touch at agreed-upon times when life leads you to different places. Being engaged means that you are committing to being the person your partner can reach out to in times of stress or joy. This is true no matter what's going on. You will want to assure each other that when one of you reaches out, the other will reach back, despite the distance.

HOW TO STAY IN TOUCH

If one of you is currently planning a trip for business or to visit family, use this worksheet to come to an agreement about when you will be in contact. If you don't have any trips planned, think up a fictitious scenario and do this exercise anyway. It will be good practice for the future.

Time zone difference: _____

Video chat _____ times per day at these times: _____

Phone call _____ times per day at these times: _____
Or phone call only in the event of emergencies: _____

Emails whenever we think of something we want to share, but we don't expect an immediate response.

Texts are okay between the hours of _____ and _____.

Partner Discussion
Discuss the realities of how frequently you can be in touch when you're not together. Accept that you are both going to be on your own doing your own thing. Maybe you will video chat in the evening before bed and speak on the phone in the morning. Maybe you'll video chat all day long. Whatever works for both of you to keep your connection strong without putting too much pressure on each other is the best way forward. Try to get on the same page before either of you goes away.

_____

_____

_____

_____

GIVE AND GET FEEDBACK

Even when you are both deeply connected and can sometimes accurately guess what's going on in the other's mind, you are still two people who need to give and get feedback to keep moving forward in your relationship. Don't fall into the habit of taking your intimate relationship for granted and assuming that all is well without regular check-ins. Yes, good intentions count, but are your good intentions conveying the right amount of admiration and affection you feel for your partner? Are you expressing your love and respect often enough?

Sometimes our partners will miss the best of what we offer because we don't take the extra step. The next time you want to tell your partner how much you appreciate them, pause and touch your partner's arm. Tell your partner something you appreciate about what they did. For example, say something like, "I want to tell you something. I really want you to take it in. I cannot tell you how much I appreciate the way you [fill in the blank]. It means so much to me. I don't know how I could have handled that without you. Thank you." Conveying your love and gratitude like this cannot be overlooked. It shows you appreciate all the efforts your partner has put into being there for you.

In the space provided, fashion a heartfelt statement about something your partner did that you deeply appreciate.

> **PARTNER A**

_____
_____
_____
_____
_____

> **PARTNER B**

_____
_____
_____
_____
_____

Partner Discussion

Share your statements with each other. When it is your turn to say your statement, touch your partner and look into their eyes. End with a heartfelt thank you. As the receiving partner, offer feedback on your partner's statement. Make thanking each other for the things you appreciate a habit that lasts a lifetime.

Discussion Notes

_____
_____
_____
_____
_____

SEXUAL INTIMACY

You may have already experienced the delicious joy that accompanies a sexual experience together, or you may be abstaining from sex until you are married. If you are looking forward to a first-time sexual experience on your wedding night, plan for that moment with anticipation as well as with care. You may have built it up to be such a momentous occasion that reality can't live up to it. Just be mindful of all that has gone down during the day and allow for the potential tiredness that may make the experience a little less than paradise. Know you have a future of sexual encounters to experience from that night on.

Whatever your current situation is, I want to underline the importance of having regular sex in your relationship. Without some form of deep romantic and sexual intimacy, you will feel like roommates. Nothing will bring you closer than taking the time to relax into mutual pleasuring. Sharing intense erotic moments will become a quintessential ingredient of your relationship. That bonded feeling will give your relationship the extended lasting sense of oneness that will undergird your love for each other.

SHARE YOUR SEXUAL PREFERENCES

Even if you are currently engaging in sex, there's a good chance there's still a lot you need to learn about your partner in the bedroom. Read the statements that follow and place a checkmark in the box that best represents your preferences and desires. Then respond to the prompts. Review your responses together and have a playful conversation around them.

PARTNER A

STATEMENT	MAYBE	SOMETIMES	NEVER
I LOVE IT WHEN YOU INITIATE OUR SEXUAL INTIMACY.			
I WANT US BOTH TO FEEL FREE TO INITIATE SEXUAL INTIMACY.			
I ENJOY TELLING YOU ABOUT SOME OF MY FANTASIES AND MIGHT BE UP FOR ACTING SOME OF THEM OUT.			

STATEMENT	MAYBE	SOMETIMES	NEVER
I SOMETIMES WILL WANT TO MIX IT UP AND HAVE SEX IN PLACES OTHER THAN OUR BEDROOM.			
I LOVE TO CUDDLE AFTER SEX AND JUST ENJOY THE AFTERMATH OF OUR PASSION.			
I LOVE IT WHEN YOU MAKE APPROVING NOISES WHEN SOMETHING FEELS GOOD.			
I WOULD ENJOY MAKING A RITUAL OF HAVING SEX AND PUT IT ON OUR CALENDAR.			

In this phase of our relationship, I would enjoy a frequency of sex about _____ times a _____.

Let's agree to make it a regular habit to check in about our feelings about our sex life together at least once a _____.

One signal I would enjoy using to indicate my interest in having sex with you is _____.

I am more comfortable with the lights _____.

> PARTNER B <

STATEMENT	MAYBE	SOMETIMES	NEVER
I LOVE IT WHEN YOU INITIATE OUR SEXUAL INTIMACY.			
I WANT US BOTH TO FEEL FREE TO INITIATE SEXUAL INTIMACY.			
I ENJOY TELLING YOU ABOUT SOME OF MY FANTASIES AND MIGHT BE UP FOR ACTING SOME OF THEM OUT.			
I SOMETIMES WILL WANT TO MIX IT UP AND HAVE SEX IN PLACES OTHER THAN OUR BEDROOM.			
I LOVE TO CUDDLE AFTER SEX AND JUST ENJOY THE AFTERMATH OF OUR PASSION.			
I LOVE IT WHEN YOU MAKE APPROVING NOISES WHEN SOMETHING FEELS GOOD.			
I WOULD ENJOY MAKING A RITUAL OF HAVING SEX AND PUT IT ON OUR CALENDAR.			

In this phase of our relationship, I would enjoy a frequency of sex about _____ times a _____.

Let's agree to make it a regular habit to check in about our feelings about our sex life together at least once a _____.

One signal I would enjoy using to indicate my interest in having sex with you is _____.

I am more comfortable with the lights _____.

Share your responses with each other and note where your desires come together or diverge. Talk about how you can accommodate both your wishes.

Discussion Notes

_____

_____

_____

_____

_____

EXPECTATIONS AROUND INTIMACY

In the beginning of your relationship, you may think your expectations for being close and intimate are in sync. And they probably are. But during this process, you may also be learning new things about what your partner imagines will happen after you are married. Bringing your expectations out in the open now and agreeing on what's realistic is a great step for heading into your future together. Now's the time to practice harmonizing any expectations that don't line up.

MUTUAL AGREEMENTS AROUND SEX

Discuss the following statements to determine where you both stand:

1. Either partner can say, "Not now" if you do not feel like responding to a sexual overture, but you will set a future time when you would more likely enjoy the experience.
2. Either partner can pleasure themselves in private and use erotic material if they wish.
3. When your partner has a desire for sex but you are not quite into it, you will still bring your partner to orgasm.
4. Pain is to be avoided during sex. If either partner feels discomfort, they will share it with the other. (Many partners feel like they should bear it but it would be smart to check in with a doctor. Never underestimate the value of extra lubrication.)

As you review each of these statements, see how you feel and notice if you get stuck talking about it. Sexual issues can sometimes push hot buttons. Try to support and understand your partner's feelings of vulnerability, as well as your own.

HOW MUCH TIME?

Rank the importance of each of the different forms of intimacy listed in this worksheet on a scale from 1 (low) to 5 (high). Also fill in how much time you would like to devote each day or week to that activity. You'll have an opportunity to discuss your responses after you've completed this worksheet.

FREQUENCY	PARTNER A	PARTNER B
TIME TO CATCH UP WITH EACH OTHER TO KNOW WHAT'S REALLY GOING ON IN YOUR DAY		
TIME FOR SHARING IDEAS ABOUT WHAT'S GOING ON IN THE WORLD		

FREQUENCY	PARTNER A	PARTNER B
TIME FOR MUTUAL ACTIVITIES, LIKE SPORTS, MOVIES, TV, ETC.		
TIME FOR PHYSICAL EXERCISE OR WALKS IN NATURE		
TIME FOR CUDDLING AND HOLDING		
TIME FOR SEX		

Partner Discussion

Look for places where your circles of interest overlap and start there. Then acknowledge places where your expectations do not match. If necessary, look for trade-offs that would make you both feel heard and where you each are getting something you want. Schedule times to review your expectations and to call to each other's attention what is or is not working.

Discussion Notes

_____

_____

_____

_____

_____

SEXUAL DESIRES

As a kid, you were probably taught the difference between wanting something and needing something. You had to learn that just because you desperately felt you had to have it did not mean you needed it. Similarly, treat your desires as yearnings but not as "have to" demands.

When it comes to sexual intimacy, you will want to take the opportunity to tease out the nuances of what you feel most relaxed doing and ask for it. Touch on these areas to see if you have any hot spots to work through. Identify where you fall on this continuum by marking the point for each set of statements that best describes you. You'll have a chance to discuss your responses after you've each marked your points on the continuums.

Feel Shy Around Sex   Feel Relaxed Sexually

● ● ● ● ● ● ● ● ● ● ●

Sex Once or Twice a Month   Sex Once or Twice a Day

● ● ● ● ● ● ● ● ● ● ●

Missionary Position   Varied Sexual Positions

● ● ● ● ● ● ● ● ● ● ●

Lights Off   Lights On

● ● ● ● ● ● ● ● ● ● ●

"Vanilla" Forms of Sexual Expression   Up for Anything

● ● ● ● ● ● ● ● ● ● ●

Feel Shy Around Sex   Feel Relaxed Sexually

● ● ● ● ● ● ● ● ● ● ●

Sex Once or Twice a Month   Sex Once or Twice a Day

● ● ● ● ● ● ● ● ● ● ●

Missionary Position   Varied Sexual Positions

● ● ● ● ● ● ● ● ● ● ●

Lights Off   Lights On

● ● ● ● ● ● ● ● ● ● ●

"Vanilla" Forms of Sexual Expression   Up for Anything

● ● ● ● ● ● ● ● ● ● ●

Partner Discussion

Discuss the points where you are in alignment. Where you are not in alignment, approach the discussion with compassion and curiosity. Try to learn more about why your partner feels the way they do.

Discussion Notes

_____

_____

_____

_____

_____

PRACTICE ASKING FOR WHAT YOU WANT

You will achieve a level of psychological maturity when you ask for (but not demand) what you need and yearn for in your intimate relationship. Take turns completing the follow phrases out loud:

I would love it if you . . .

It would mean so much to me if you . . .

I would get excited if you . . .

Partner Discussion

Notice how these statements are phrased to express something you would like. You aren't asking, "How come you never [fill in the blank]?" or, "You always do [fill in the blank] rather than [fill in the blank]." That approach only puts your partner on the defensive and makes them feel wrong. Discuss how it felt to ask for what you want and how it felt to be on the receiving end of the request.

Discussion Notes

_____

_____

_____

_____

_____

BOUNDARIES AROUND INTIMACY

To feel safe in your relationship, both partners need to articulate what does and does not make them feel comfortable. Agreeing to discuss limits around intimacy is a further step in getting to know each other and finding out what each of you prefers. Basically, establishing what works for you will help you feel safer rather than having the sense that you're walking on eggshells. Notice when you are not feeling respected and use that as an opportunity to talk about boundaries. Appreciate the absolute necessity of protecting that positive glow and admiration you feel toward each other.

There are certain aspects of your intimate life that you may not want your partner to share with others. You may not want photos of your intimate dinner together posted on social media. You may want some time alone occasionally. You may want to keep details about your sex life to yourself. You may want bathroom time to be completely private. It's important to lay out what you find acceptable and unacceptable.

ARTICULATE YOUR BOUNDARIES

In the following worksheet, place a checkmark next to all of the items that are true for you and add any of your own. After you've both done this, you'll have an opportunity to discuss.

- [ ] I do not enjoy being interrupted when I am concentrating.
- [ ] I need _____ minutes of alone time when I come home from work or school.
- [ ] I feel uncomfortable when you insist on knowing what I'm thinking.
- [ ] I do not want you to grab me from behind when I am doing something.
- [ ] I do not want you to approach me for sex when I'm upset.
- [ ] I want to be able to interrupt you when what you are saying is boring to me.
- [ ] I do not want to discuss issues we are having before bed.
- [ ] I want you to keep details about our relationship private from friends and family.
- [ ] I do not want you to tell me what to do.
- [ ] I do not want you to put me down in front of other people.
- [ ] I do not want you to post pictures on social media of me without my consent.
- [ ] _____
- [ ] _____
- [ ] _____
- [ ] _____

- [ ] I do not enjoy being interrupted when I am concentrating.
- [ ] I need _____ minutes of alone time when I come home from work or school.
- [ ] I feel uncomfortable when you insist on knowing what I'm thinking.
- [ ] I do not want you to grab me from behind when I am doing something.
- [ ] I do not want you to approach me for sex when I'm upset.
- [ ] I want to be able to interrupt you when what you are saying is boring to me.
- [ ] I do not want to discuss issues we are having before bed.
- [ ] I want you to keep details about our relationship private from friends and family.

- [ ] I do not want you to tell me what to do.
- [ ] I do not want you to put me down in front of other people.
- [ ] I do not want you to post pictures on social media of me without my consent.
- [ ] _____
- [ ] _____
- [ ] _____

Partner Discussion

Do any of your partner's boundaries surprise you? If you feel like a boundary your partner is asking for is unreasonable, have a conversation to bring to light why they feel that way. Promise to do your best to comply with the boundaries they are requesting. Be aware that this list you just created may not cover everything that will come up, and more boundaries may need to be established. The fine art of setting boundaries requires you to find the right time and place to talk about them. Agree to avoid bringing up the topic of boundary-setting when either of you is feeling angry or slighted.

Discussion Notes

_____

_____

_____

_____

_____

EXTRAMARITAL RELATIONSHIPS

You will probably make a vow at your wedding to forsake all others. Most premarital couples hesitate to explore this topic because it seems inconceivable at this stage that you would ever cheat on each other. Start by recognizing the prevalence of extramarital relationships in our culture. When you hear of it, even in the lives of celebrities, let it serve as a wake-up call to check in with each other to affirm your commitment to be there for each other only.

If either of you notices you are feeling drawn to someone (including the possibility of emotional infidelity), promise to discuss it with your partner and reaffirm your commitment. You can use it as an opportunity to evaluate if any needs are not being met in your present relationship.

In my experience as a marriage counselor, no partner can anticipate the tsunami or trauma that the betrayal of an affair can create. So promise each other you will get into therapy before beginning an affair. Should you discover an affair has happened, here's the good news: When couples seek help after infidelity, they can not only recover but also construct a level of intimacy they may not have known before.

While it takes quite a while to rebuild trust, the effort will bear fruit in restoring faith that you can count on the other. Be sure to reach out to a therapist who specializes in extramarital affair recovery.

An Emotional Affair

I want to include an angle you might not have thought about regarding your commitment to forsake all others. Sometimes, if you and your partner are having problems, you may find yourself wanting to talk to someone to vent to or ask for advice. You may at times turn to a wise person to explore some of your feelings. This may include a counselor, a clergy person, or someone you both admire. However, sharing your problems with someone to whom you could potentially feel an attraction is a dangerous step. If you find yourself doing this, listen to the warning bells and find an alternate person to confide in. What may seem innocent at first opens a door to a level of intimacy with someone who is not your partner.

EXPLORE WHAT IT MEANS TO BE UNFAITHFUL

Spend a few minutes thinking about what being unfaithful to one's partner in marriage means to you as a general concept. Think about what you've experienced or witnessed that has shaped your sense about it. Do you know anyone who went through it? If so, what impression did it leave on you? In the space provided, free write anything that comes to mind around infidelity. Once you've both done this, move on to the partner discussion.

> **PARTNER A**

_____

_____

_____

_____

_____

> **PARTNER B**

_____

_____

_____

_____

_____

Partner Discussion

Share with each other what you have written and allow this to lead into a serious, heartfelt conversation regarding your thoughts and feelings about infidelity. Commit to closing any doors or windows that might lead to an outside relationship long before it gets off the ground. Promise yourselves that you will seek out a marriage counselor if your mind starts drifting away from your partner and toward someone else. Also, as unbelievable as it is right now, agree that if infidelity does happen in your marriage, you will seek help together.

Discussion Notes

_____

_____

_____

_____

COUPLE CHECK-IN

Flip back through this chapter and review your responses to the exercises. Were there any sticking points that one or both of you would like to revisit and work on more? What were your three biggest takeaways from this part of the workbook? Take notes in the spaces provided and discuss the items you've listed. Make an agreement to return to the exercises you would like to work further on before moving ahead to the next chapter.

▸ PARTNER A ◂

Exercises I would like to work on more:

_____

_____

_____

_____

_____

My three biggest takeaways were:

1. _____

2. _____

3. _____

▸ PARTNER B ◂

Exercises I would like to work on more:

_____

_____

_____

_____

_____

My three biggest takeaways were:

1. _____

2. _____

3. _____

ACTION ITEMS

1. Take turns planning an intimate experience. Surprise your partner by only specifying the time and what to wear.

2. Keeping boundaries in mind, think up an erotic experience the two of you can share, either now or after you are married.

3. Sign up for tango lessons. This type of dance is intimate and requires one partner to take the lead from the other and then move in sync.

4. Spend an evening simply touching and holding each other. Connect to your senses of taste, touch, sight, and smell to enhance the experience. Use candles and soft lighting. Stay aware in each moment and savor your time together.

5. Take a shower together and enjoy the sensuousness of washing each other's body or take a bubble bath in candlelight and play soft music.

CHAPTER

5

Children

SO FAR, THIS WORKBOOK has focused on the experiences that can strengthen your relationship as a unit of two. Eventually, you may add some more people into the mix: children. But the first question to ask is: Are you drawn to the role of parenthood? Not everyone feels a maternal or paternal urge. Hopefully, you and your partner have already discussed whether or not you eventually want to have children. Maybe this is still up in the air for one or both of you. If that's the case, this chapter, which explores the dynamics of the decision to become a parent, can help you gain clarity.

For many, the arrival of your first child will stand out as the most exhilarating bonding experience you can have. You may find yourselves wanting to play the "Hallelujah" chorus over and over as I did when my daughter arrived. That child's total dependency on you will win your hearts in a flash. Coming home to your child's smile will brighten your heart daily, and reaching out to get a hug from that little person can give you a new sense of meaning for the rest of your life.

With all that said, children don't come without challenges. Some couples say that their marital satisfaction took a tumble after their kids came. It's not unusual. However, working through these exercises can help you develop the habit of staying in touch as a couple as you bring children into the world. One of the greatest gifts you can offer your children comes from exactly what you are doing with this workbook. Your youngsters will blossom when you have built the solid bond you are creating through this work.

NUMBER AND TIMING

Let's talk about whether you want children and how many. You will want to ferret out each other's wishes and begin to plan the size of family you wish to have. Start by writing down how many children were in your family.

Partner A: _____

Partner B: _____

Discuss with each other whether the size of your family of origin feels like the ideal family size to you. If you grew up as one of six children but your partner was an only child, you each might have a different idea of how many children makes the ideal family.

When you're just starting out and you're thinking about adding one or more children to your lives, you might rightfully feel concerned about the long-term impact *six* children (or any children) will have on your finances. In 2017, the U.S. Department of Agriculture issued a report estimating that the total cost to raise one child to age 17 in the United States is currently $233,610 (not including college). Even if six feels like the ideal number to you and you remember all the fun you had growing up with lots of brothers and sisters, you need to be sure that you will have the finances to keep them happy, safe, and comfortable.

HOW MANY CHILDREN DO YOU WANT?

Be totally honest here. It's important to be straightforward about what you expect with regard to children. If you do not want any and don't think you will change your mind later on, be sure to express this now.

I want _____ children.

I want _____ children.

Partner Discussion

Are you in alignment with the number of children you want or are you way off? If you find that you are in disagreement, ask your partner to express why they long for the size family they do. Is there any room for compromise? When it comes to children, you will need to get on the same page.

Discussion Notes

_____

_____

_____

_____

_____

HOW LONG WILL YOU WAIT?

Regarding when you want your first child, many couples report that they were so glad that they did not have a child for the first two years of their marriage. This gave them time to create a solid foundation and bond so that the stress of parenting did not shake their connection to each other.

Part A: When to Have Your First Child

Choose the response in the following worksheet that best reflects when you would like to start trying to get pregnant.

	RIGHT AWAY	IN A FEW YEARS	WHEN WE ARE TOTALLY SECURE IN OUR PROFESSIONS
PARTNER A			
PARTNER B			

Part B: When to Have Your Next Child

Assuming you and your partner wish to have a second child, choose the response in the following worksheet that best reflects your desires. Do this for as many children as you have agreed to have. If you want to plan your family size carefully, you might be interested in the Mayo Clinic's recommendation: To reduce risk of pregnancy complications, attempt your next pregnancy after 18 months and before five years following your last healthy pregnancy.

	CLOSELY TOGETHER	TWO YEARS APART	MANY YEARS APART
PARTNER A			
PARTNER B			

Partner Discussion

Talk about how various pulls in your life may affect when you have your first child and any subsequent children. Listen again to any longing that is connected to your partner's choices and ask for stories that might have created the vision they have been holding. If you are very different in your desires, work together to come up with a compromise that feels like a win-win.

_____

_____

_____

_____

_____

CONSIDERING NOT HAVING CHILDREN?

There's a case for not having children that one or both of you may have considered. Many couples feel committed to demanding careers that don't leave room for raising a family or they wonder if their income will sufficiently cover the costs of childcare with enough left over to make it worth leaving young children in someone else's care.

In the United States, maternity leave and paternity leave are not guaranteed. This is an important consideration for those whose financial situation cannot cover lost pay. If you are considering not bringing children of your own into the world, this might be why. Perhaps there are other reasons you haven't considered. The next exercise will help you explore what those might be.

EXPLORE REASONS FOR NOT HAVING CHILDREN

In the following worksheet, check the box that most describes how you feel for each statement. You'll have an opportunity to compare notes with your partner after you have both completed the exercise.

STATEMENT	NOT CONCERNING	A LITTLE CONCERNING	VERY CONCERNING
I SOMETIMES WORRY ABOUT GIVING UP CONTROL OF MY LIFE AND MY CAREER IF WE HAVE CHILDREN.			
I AM DEDICATED TO MY CAREER AND DO NOT WANT TO JEOPARDIZE MY CHANCE FOR SUCCESS BY HAVING A CHILD.			
WITH ALL OF THE PROBLEMS IN THE WORLD, I AM NOT COMFORTABLE BRINGING A CHILD INTO THE WORLD.			
I WANT THE OPPORTUNITY TO TRAVEL AND SPEND A LOT OF RECREATIONAL TIME WITH MY PARTNER. I AM CONCERNED THAT HAVING A CHILD WOULD MAKE THAT IMPOSSIBLE.			
OTHER:			

PARTNER B

STATEMENT	NOT CONCERNING	A LITTLE CONCERNING	VERY CONCERNING
I SOMETIMES WORRY ABOUT GIVING UP CONTROL OF MY LIFE AND MY CAREER IF WE HAVE CHILDREN.			
I AM DEDICATED TO MY CAREER AND DO NOT WANT TO JEOPARDIZE MY CHANCE FOR SUCCESS BY HAVING A CHILD.			
WITH ALL OF THE PROBLEMS IN THE WORLD, I AM NOT COMFORTABLE BRINGING A CHILD INTO THE WORLD.			
I WANT THE OPPORTUNITY TO TRAVEL AND SPEND A LOT OF RECREATIONAL TIME WITH MY PARTNER. I AM CONCERNED THAT HAVING A CHILD WOULD MAKE THAT IMPOSSIBLE.			
OTHER:			

Partner Discussion

Discuss your responses to these statements. Notice where you are in alignment and where you differ. Be open to hearing your partner's perspective and try to understand why they feel the way they do. Brainstorm ways to alleviate concerns if one of you wants children but the other does not.

Discussion Notes

_____

_____

_____

_____

_____

IMAGINE YOUR FUTURE

Describe what you imagine your life will be like 10 years from now if you didn't have any children:

> PARTNER A <

_____

_____

_____

_____

_____

_____

_____

_____

_____

_____

Describe what you imagine your life will be like 10 years from now if you had one or more children:

PARTNER A

_____

_____

_____

_____

_____

PARTNER B

_____

_____

_____

_____

_____

Partner Discussion

Read each other's descriptions and ask for more details until you both have a complete picture of what you each envision will happen if you do and do not have children. Approach this with curiosity and without judgment. The future is not written in stone; you can work as a team to make it what you want it to be—together.

_____

_____

_____

_____

_____

CHILDREN BY ANOTHER MARRIAGE

One (or even both) of you may bring into your marriage children from another marriage or relationship. If so, you are entering a ready-made family. Obviously, if you are the partner who doesn't have children, you will be inheriting deep involvement in your stepchildren's lives. If you have never experienced parenthood, you may not find yourself prepared for the depth of loyalty your partner feels toward their children, sometimes at the expense of time spent with you. At times, you may feel torn between your partner's needs to be there for their children and your wish to have your partner be there for you.

Marriage counselors know that this can be one of the most complex and challenging dynamics for a new marriage. However, if you use the tools and skills you are developing in this workbook, you and your partner will stay connected by sharing meaningful time apart from the kids. Express your yearning for anything that is missing from your relationship, and at the same time listen to your partner's struggles and frustrations regarding a blended family. When you both speak from the heart, you will feel compassion for each other and work together to arrive at a win-win solution.

PARENTING STYLES

While you are discussing the possibility of having kids, you'll want to also consider what kind of parent you each want to be to your children. Psychologists have delineated four styles of parenting:

WHAT IF?

With all of this talk about whether or not you want to have children, there's the matter of actually getting pregnant once you decide you want to have a baby. The good news is that after six months of trying, 60 percent of couples will conceive, and on average, 85 to 90 percent of couples who have unprotected sex will get pregnant in a year, according to Pregnancy-Info.net. This site further states that if the reproductive system is functioning well, 20 percent of women in their twenties who are having unprotected sex will get pregnant in just the first month.

On the other hand, according to Resolve, the National Infertility Association, one in eight couples will have trouble getting pregnant or sustaining a pregnancy. Those over age 35 may have more difficulty conceiving. According to the Mayo Clinic, women in their mid-thirties begin to have more fertility problems than their younger counterparts. Of course, science has created many ways to treat infertility, but these procedures can be costly.

Some couples may choose to adopt. Many adoptive parents report that their feelings of attachment grew quickly and that they felt proud to have given a child an opportunity to experience the love of family. Have an open and honest discussion with each other surrounding your feelings about adoption. For now, it's just a simple discussion to see where you both stand on the idea of bringing a child into your home who is related by love rather than by blood.

1. Authoritarian Parenting Style

This style is basically the "because I say so" approach. These parents tend to assume that children need to be told exactly what to do. They provide a firm structure and hold a child to it and expect them to obey the rules. These parents tend to have very high expectations. They often do not accompany these with much warmth and support. They treat mistakes as big deals to be punished harshly, either physically or verbally. They may have very little patience. Children may be left with a sense that there is something wrong with them. Children of authoritarian parents often feel they have no room to negotiate. They might feel frustrated at having to give in to their parents' wishes.

2. Authoritative Parenting Style

This style gives the child the sense that parents really care. They set limits while explaining the reasons why. These parents allow expression of a point of view during decision-making. They tend to foster independence and promote learning how to make good decisions. They set fair rules, and punishment is reasonable. A child knows what to expect if they break the rules. These parents offer flexibility and warmth. They seek to be parents who work with their offspring. The children may grow up with a sense that they are loved just the way they are.

3. Uninvolved Parenting Style

These parents seem to be uninterested or even neglectful. When they talk to their children, they may still be looking at their phone, computer, television, or tablet. The child never knows whether they are really listening or just pretending to listen. For a child, it may be hard to get the attention of uninvolved parents, and they may resort to screaming or other misbehavior to feel seen and heard. These parents also sometimes abuse alcohol or drugs. As a result, the child often has to fend for themselves, not knowing when it is possible to count on their parents.

4. Permissive Parenting Style

This style tends to have an "anything goes" approach. Their children often come up with their own rules and guidelines. These parents tend to be nurturing, but they want to be a friend and not take on the parental role of enforcing rules and discipline. The children don't have to worry about being punished because no consequences are imposed.

Children of parents like this often feel they have the power to wrap the adults around their finger to get what they want with tactics such as whining. When a youngster asks for help, they may walk away feeling that the parents don't know what to do to help them. These parents sometimes ask their kids what the kid should do. A child might wonder, *Who's the parent here and why did they ask me for advice?*

IDENTIFY YOUR PARENTS' STYLE

You may have recognized your own parents in one or more of the descriptions. If each of your parents had a different style, you may have had to learn to shift gears depending on which parent was in charge. Reflect on the role models of your childhood. Circle either "mother" or "father" for each of the parenting styles discussed that you think best describes their approach.

PARTNER A'S PARENTS		PARTNER B'S PARENTS	
AUTHORITARIAN MOTHER FATHER	AUTHORITATIVE MOTHER FATHER	AUTHORITARIAN MOTHER FATHER	AUTHORITATIVE MOTHER FATHER
UNINVOLVED MOTHER FATHER	PERMISSIVE MOTHER FATHER	UNINVOLVED MOTHER FATHER	PERMISSIVE MOTHER FATHER

Partner Discussion

Discuss how each of your parents modeled the parenting style you identified. Explore what you did and didn't like about your parents' approaches to child-rearing. Are there things about any of your parents' approaches that you want to incorporate into your life with your future children? Are there any you want to avoid? Decide as a couple which parenting approach you think will work best for each of you.

Discussion Notes

_____

_____

_____

_____

If you had to choose a set of parents that you think are doing or have done a great job raising their children, who would you each choose? If you don't just choose your own parents, spend some time imagining what you would be like if you had been raised by that couple. How would your personality be different? What might you be doing differently now? How might their influence have made a positive impact on you?

> **PARTNER A**

I admire this set of parents: _____

If they had raised me, I imagine the following would be different:

_____

_____

_____

_____

_____

> **PARTNER B**

I admire this set of parents: _____

If they had raised me, I imagine the following would be different:

_____

_____

_____

_____

_____

Partner Discussion

Describe to each other what parts of this couple's parenting style you admire and ways in which you can identify with them and model your own parenting approach after theirs. Talk about what you think would be different in your life if you had had them as parents and whether or not you could make these changes yourself.

Discussion Notes

_____

_____

_____

_____

_____

IDENTIFY OTHERS' PARENTING STYLES

The next time you visit relatives or friends with kids, pay close attention to how they interact with their children. Later, as a couple, try to identify the parenting styles they used. Describe how you think the children are impacted by their parenting approach. Do you aspire to be like them or is there something about their approach that you don't like? Jot down your observations in the space provided.

❯ PARTNER A ❮

_____

_____

_____

_____

_____

❯ PARTNER B ❮

_____

_____

_____

_____

_____

Partner Discussion

Did you notice different things about the couple's parenting styles or were you on the same page with what you witnessed? Did one of you agree with an approach that the other felt could have been handled better? Talk about your similarities and differences.

Discussion Notes

_____

_____

_____

_____

CHILDCARE RESPONSIBILITIES

Long gone are the days when it was assumed that the mother would stay at home and take care of the day-to-day needs of the children. Do you know where each of you stands with regard to childcare? This is an important discussion to have at this juncture so you aren't surprised when it's time to bring your little one home.

You may know in your heart that you are deeply committed to success in your career and don't want to stop working, or maybe you cannot wait until your first child arrives because you will be able to stay at home full time. Even if your plan falls somewhere in between, you will want to know which childcare tasks feel most natural for you and which will present a real challenge.

CHILDCARE TASKS

Look over this list as a couple and discuss which of these responsibilities are ones you want to take care of, which you want to do together, and which you prefer your partner do. Your choices are not written in stone, so go ahead and put a checkmark in the boxes that reflect what makes the most sense right now.

CHILDCARE TASK	PARTNER A RESPONSIBILITY	PARTNERS A AND B TOGETHER	PARTNER B RESPONSIBILITY
FEEDING			
SHOPPING FOR CLOTHES			
PUTTING TO BED			
CHANGING DIAPERS			
READING STORIES			
PLAYING GAMES OR ATTENDING GAMES			
OVERSEEING HOMEWORK			
LISTENING TO PROBLEMS			
CREATING PARTIES			
FOSTERING MORAL OR SPIRITUAL DEVELOPMENT			
SETTING RULES AND METING OUT DISCIPLINE			
TAKING TO THE DOCTOR AND OTHER APPOINTMENTS			
CLEANING UP AFTER MESSES			
ADD YOUR OWN	PARTNER A RESPONSIBILITY	PARTNERS A AND B TOGETHER	PARTNER B RESPONSIBILITY

The following worksheet offers a list of common obstacles people fear they will encounter when they consider the prospect of parenting. Review the list and check off any fears that resonate with you. Following this worksheet, you will have a chance to discuss these fears and respond to additional prompts.

FEARS	PARTNER A	PARTNER B
OUR WORK LIVES WILL LEAVE US WITH LITTLE TIME FOR OUR CHILDREN'S NEEDS.		
MY WAY OR MY PARTNER'S WAY OF DEALING WITH INTENSE EMOTIONS MAY NOT BE APPROPRIATE FOR OUR CHILDREN.		
MY PARTNER OR I MAY NOT APPLY DISCIPLINE CONSISTENTLY.		
MY PARTNER OR I WILL SIDE WITH THE CHILDREN WHEN THEY GET INTO TROUBLE, THUS SPOILING THEM.		
WE WILL NOT BE ABLE TO PROVIDE FINANCIALLY FOR OUR CHILDREN.		
WE WILL HAVE TROUBLE AGREEING ON AND STICKING TO REASONABLE CONSEQUENCES FOR OUR CHILDREN.		
I WILL HAVE TROUBLE RESPONDING TO THE NEEDS OF MY CHILDREN WHEN I AM BUSY.		
MY PARTNER AND I WILL DISAGREE ON THE BOUNDARIES WE SET WITH OUR FAMILIES REGARDING HOW THEY INTERACT WITH OUR CHILDREN.		
WE WILL HAVE TO PLACE OUR CHILDREN IN CHILDCARE SO WE CAN WORK TO MAKE ENDS MEET.		
MY PARTNER OR I WILL DISAGREE ON WHETHER/WHICH METHOD OF CHILDCARE IS APPROPRIATE FOR OUR CHILDREN.		
WE WILL STRUGGLE TO FIND A CHILDCARE FACILITY THAT MEETS OUR NEEDS AND IS SAFE FOR OUR CHILDREN.		
WE WILL NOT BE ABLE TO AFFORD CHILDCARE AND WILL HAVE TO ASK OUR FAMILIES FOR HELP.		
OUR FAMILIES WILL BE UNWILLING TO HELP US CARE FOR OUR CHILDREN SO THAT WE CAN WORK TO MAKE ENDS MEET.		
OUR FAMILIES WILL AGREE TO HELP CARE FOR OUR CHILDREN, BUT THEY WILL FEEL ENTITLED TO DISCIPLINE OR EDUCATE THEM IN A WAY WE FEEL IS INAPPROPRIATE OR HARMFUL.		
OUR CHILDREN WILL PREFER THE COMPANY OF THEIR TEACHERS OR OTHER CAREGIVERS OVER OUR COMPANY.		

ADD YOUR OWN	PARTNER A	PARTNER B

What steps can I undertake in my role as a parent to avoid encountering these obstacles?

_____

_____

_____

In what areas do I need to grow so I'm equipped to deal with these issues if they arise?

_____

_____

_____

In what areas will I need my partner's help to grow so we can face any obstacles as a team?

_____

_____

_____

What steps can I undertake in my role as a parent to avoid encountering these obstacles?

_____

_____

_____

In what areas do I need to grow so I'm equipped to deal with these issues if they arise?

_____

_____

_____

In what areas will I need my partner's help to grow so we can face any obstacles as a team?

_____

_____

_____

Partner Discussion

Have an open and honest discussion around your fears concerning parenthood. It's best to figure out how you'll face these fears now, before they become real obstacles. As always, be honest with each other and yourselves about your expectations.

Discussion Notes

_____

_____

_____

_____

_____

WHAT DOES DISCIPLINE MEAN TO YOU?

Let's look at discipline. In a thesaurus, you will find words like punishment, persuasion, self-control, self-restraint, regulation, and authority. When you think of disciplining your children, which of these words resonate with you? Can you think of more? Write them in the space provided:

> PARTNER A

_____

_____

> PARTNER B

_____

_____

You've probably heard the phrase, "Spare the rod and spoil the child." However, the American Academy of Pediatrics (AAP) suggests that spanking or even harsh verbal abuse will lead to your children becoming more aggressive and abusive to others later on. What are your feelings about spanking? Did you grow up in a family where physical or harsh verbal abuse was common? Would you find it a challenge to honor the AAP's recommendation not to use physical discipline or verbal abuse as punishment? Respond to these questions in the space provided:

> PARTNER A

_____

_____

> PARTNER B

_____

_____

Partner Discussion

Try to come to an agreement about what your discipline expectations are and what boundaries you feel should always be upheld. Consider what in each other's life might inform your individual disciplinary preferences. Be patient and kind as you come up with your disciplinary plan.

Discussion Notes

_____

_____

_____

_____

_____

WHAT WOULD YOU DO IF . . . ?

My wife has been a kindergarten teacher for 20 years. She says to her students, "I won't let you harm yourself, harm someone else, or harm the environment." You might want to use that approach when deciding whether or not you need to step in and discipline your child. As you explore your future style of parenting, write down how you think you each might respond to the following scenarios:

Your child is having a fight with another child, either verbal or physical.

> PARTNER A

I would:

_____

> PARTNER B

I would:

_____

Your child continually interrupts the two of you while you are having a conversation.

PARTNER A

I would:

_____

PARTNER B

I would:

_____

Your child isn't keeping common areas clean.

PARTNER A

I would:

_____

PARTNER B

I would:

_____

Your child refuses to do their homework.

PARTNER A

I would:

_____

PARTNER B

I would:

_____

Your child is frustrated and wants to give up on something important.

I would:

_____

I would:

_____

Partner Discussion

Discuss whether or not you would approach these common problems in a similar way. If not, discuss the differences to try to understand why each of you responded as you did. Is it because your parents would have reacted that way? Explore alternative ways to respond to these scenarios as individuals and as a team.

Discussion Notes

_____

_____

_____

_____

_____

WHAT ARE THE CONSEQUENCES?

Consequences should be age-appropriate. What might make sense for a teenager wouldn't make sense for a two-year-old. There will be plenty of time for you to read, learn, and speak with professionals about what is or isn't appropriate. But to start getting a feel for where you stand with regard to punishing a child, try to come up with a joint agreement on what the consequences would be if your seven-year-old did any of the following:

Did not do their homework:
Consequence:

Lied to you:
Consequence:

Talked back to a teacher:
Consequence:

Used crayons all over the wall:
Consequence:

Hit another child:
Consequence:

IF YOUR PARENTING STYLES DON'T MATCH

After doing these exercises, you may discover that you have different perspectives on how to help your children develop the habits and self-discipline you desire for them. You are probably aware of how quickly children learn to divide and conquer, and they will often go to the most lenient parent first. At times, you may disagree about how strict you want to be with your children. Discuss whether or not you plan to present a united front even when you have different opinions about how to respond to a situation.

Do you want to set clear guidelines that you both agree on that will help you avoid this issue? If you disagree, do you want to reserve those conversations for when your child is out of earshot? It might feel premature to have this discussion, but being in a good space with each other with regard to how you will approach parenting is an important agreement to work out before you walk down the aisle.

_____

_____

_____

_____

_____

CHILDCARE

Perhaps your ideal parenting vision includes one of you staying home to raise your children. Or maybe you'll outsource your childcare. The following questions will help you set your expectations around that possibility. Respond to the following as a couple:

Do you expect your parents to help out with childcare?

_____

What does your parents' help look like? Will they care for your child themselves or will they contribute financially to childcare costs?

_____

Will you hire a babysitter, nanny, or live-in help and for what ages?

_____

What daycare or preschool will be available and how comfortable will each of you be with that?

_____

What childcare options are each of you comfortable with? Which options do you feel particularly uncomfortable with? Where do you agree with each other?

_____

_____

_____

_____

_____

Partner Discussion

Discuss the possibilities that make sense to both of you. Also discuss what concessions you'd be willing to make in terms of finances, time with your children, or your career path to achieve your career and parenting goals.

Discussion Notes

_____

_____

_____

_____

_____

EDUCATION

Parents often pick the location for their home based on a good school district. If this is important to you, you'll want to take this into consideration when choosing where to live. Take time to share your vision of the kind of education you each want for your children. Compare notes about the importance you each place on different types of school environments. If you work with a financial planner as you start your life as a married couple, they can help you factor college into your long-term savings plan.

When it comes to your children's education, figure out what sort of educational experiences you want them to have. Check off any items you think are important to give them the best education. You might base your responses on the privileges you had or didn't have when you were younger. You will have a chance to compare your answers after you've both completed the worksheet.

PARTNER A

- ☐ I want my child to be homeschooled.
- ☐ I want my child to attend a public school.
- ☐ I want my child to attend a private school.
- ☐ I want my child to attend a parochial school.
- ☐ I want my child to receive tutoring in difficult or special subjects.
- ☐ I want my child to attend after-school programs.
- ☐ I want my child to go to summer camp.
- ☐ I want to take my child to museums.
- ☐ I want my child to participate in sports.
- ☐ I want my child to take art, music, or dance lessons.
- ☐ I want to travel with my child to promote their breadth of experience.
- ☐ I want my child to learn a second language.
- ☐ Other:
- ☐ Other:

PARTNER B

- ☐ I want my child to be homeschooled.
- ☐ I want my child to attend a public school.
- ☐ I want my child to attend a private school.
- ☐ I want my child to attend a parochial school.
- ☐ I want my child to receive tutoring in difficult or special subjects.
- ☐ I want my child to attend after-school programs.
- ☐ I want my child to go to summer camp.
- ☐ I want to take my child to museums.

☐ I want my child to participate in sports.

☐ I want my child to take art, music, or dance lessons.

☐ I want to travel with my child to promote their breadth of experience.

☐ I want my child to learn a second language.

☐ Other:

☐ Other:

Partner Discussion

You may feel happily surprised by how close your answers align. If so, celebrate that you have similar values. If you find yourselves in different camps, tell stories from your past to help your partner understand your feelings around your schooling choices. Listen with curiosity and validate how these choices could feel relevant to your partner.

Discussion Notes

_____

_____

_____

_____

_____

EXPECTATIONS OF YOUR CHILDREN

You've made a lot of progress through this chapter by recalling your parents' styles of parenting, how you each want to approach parenting your children, and formulating your vision of how you will parent together. The last thing on the agenda is addressing your expectations of your future children. Research shows that parents who have high hopes for their children's achievements help them do better in life. However, having absurdly high expectations can do more harm than good. Naturally you want your children to be successful, but what does success mean to you?

CLARIFY YOUR EXPECTATIONS

Discuss your answers to the following questions to start building a sense of what you each expect from your children. There's no need to write down your responses here. Instead, use these questions as talking points and give each one discussion time and attention until you both have an idea of where you stand. You'll find space at the end to jot down any important takeaways you want to remember regarding this discussion.

1. Do you want your child to be successful academically, socially, and financially? Is one more important than the other?
2. What kinds of pressures did you experience from your parents to achieve success?
3. Are you willing to push your child to be all that they can be? If so, what does that look like?
4. How can you work as a team to encourage your child to rise to your standards for success?
5. As you think about your child's success, are you factoring in their happiness?
6. Do you expect your child to place happiness in their family above all else?

Discussion Notes

_____

_____

_____

_____

_____

COUPLE CHECK-IN

Flip back through this chapter and review your responses to the exercises. Were there any sticking points that one or both of you would like to revisit and work on more? What were your three biggest takeaways from this part of the workbook? Take notes in the spaces provided and discuss the items you've listed. Make an agreement to return to the exercises you would like to work further on before moving ahead to the next chapter.

> **PARTNER A**

Exercises I would like to work on more:

_____

_____

_____

_____

_____

My three biggest takeaways were:

1. _____

2. _____

3. _____

> **PARTNER B**

Exercises I would like to work on more:

_____

_____

_____

_____

_____

My three biggest takeaways were:

1. _____

2. _____

3. _____

ACTION ITEMS

1. Search "baby names" on Google to identify names each of you likes. Go ahead and include some crazy choices to tickle your funny bones.

2. Come up with a fictitious scenario of a child misbehaving and role-play what it would have been like if you were the child and your parents were responding to your behavior. This can convey to your partner what it was like for you to grow up with the best and worst sides of your parents. Take turns.

3. Go through some children's magazines and cut out pictures and words. Paste them onto a piece of cardboard to create a collage. Choose pictures and words that shimmer for you when you think about having children. Share your collages when they're finished.

4. Watch a sitcom or movie that portrays parenting challenges. Afterward, discuss the behaviors you saw in the children and the parents and whether or not you can relate to them.

5. Spend time with children you know—a niece or nephew, perhaps. Take them someplace fun as a couple and talk about your experiences later.

CHAPTER

6

Beliefs and Values

IF COMMUNICATION CONSTITUTES THE lifeblood of any relationship, your beliefs and values shape your everyday decisions to build a meaningful marriage. Understanding what drives you and your partner to be all that you can be creates a bond between you. An appreciation of each other's values allows you to support each other and set your intentions to grow and become better people.

In marriage, you need to listen carefully to the nuances of what your partner believes. You will want to build your "couple spirit" by striving to nurture each other's search for meaning. In this chapter, I invite you to tease out your values as well as assess the intensity of your commitment to these values. I also encourage you to become acquainted with the moral compass that guides each of you in your decision-making.

Taking a long loving look at your values and comparing them to your partner's values is an essential ingredient of any premarital counseling process. You will feel closer just knowing what makes your partner tick. By understanding the passions that drive your partner, you will feel like you know even more deeply the person with whom you are walking down the aisle.

MORALS AND VALUES

First, let's make a distinction between morals and values. When you grow up in any given culture, you are given rules that determine what people around you consider to be right and wrong. These morals serve as external guidelines that teach you how to discern the codes of ethical behavior. As you make decisions following these codes, you gain the approval of others who hold the same morals in high regard.

In contrast, you create your own personal set of values. Your values stem from what you have come to consider the right way for you to live your life. They become your internal guiding principles. You form a vision of the future to which you aspire and the action steps needed to get there. For example, you may have a moral commitment to being honest. However, if you are faced with hurting someone's feelings by telling them the truth, you may tell a white lie. That is one of your values.

IDENTIFY YOUR MORALS

This worksheet includes a sampling of morals with space to add a few of your own. Check the column that best applies to you. You'll have an opportunity to discuss your choices after you've both completed this exercise.

> PARTNER A

MORALS	VERY IMPORTANT	MODERATELY IMPORTANT	NOT IMPORTANT
BE FAITHFUL			
BE HONEST AND TRUSTWORTHY			
BE LOYAL TO FAMILY			
BE LOYAL TO FRIENDS			
CARE FOR THE VULNERABLE AND WEAK			
DON'T JUDGE OTHERS			
DON'T STEAL			

MORALS	VERY IMPORTANT	MODERATELY IMPORTANT	NOT IMPORTANT
GIVE TO THE NEEDY			
RESPECT AUTHORITY			
SELF-SACRIFICE FOR GREATER GOOD			
ADD YOUR OWN	VERY IMPORTANT	MODERATELY IMPORTANT	NOT IMPORTANT

PARTNER B

MORALS	VERY IMPORTANT	MODERATELY IMPORTANT	NOT IMPORTANT
BE FAITHFUL			
BE HONEST AND TRUSTWORTHY			
BE LOYAL TO FAMILY			
BE LOYAL TO FRIENDS			
CARE FOR THE VULNERABLE AND WEAK			
DON'T JUDGE OTHERS			
DON'T STEAL			
GIVE TO THE NEEDY			
RESPECT AUTHORITY			
SELF-SACRIFICE FOR GREATER GOOD			
ADD YOUR OWN	VERY IMPORTANT	MODERATELY IMPORTANT	NOT IMPORTANT

Partner Discussion

When you compare your responses, remember that you do not have to agree on everything. What matters is that you respect your partner's choices. Keep in mind that you will get to know your partner even more deeply by exploring why they hold certain morals in such high regard.

Discussion Notes

_____

_____

_____

_____

_____

CLARIFY YOUR VALUES

This worksheet includes a list of values with space to add others. Each partner will have an opportunity to identify whether or not a value is important to them personally. If a value is important to you, rank its importance on a scale from 1 (low) to 5 (high). If it's not important to you at all, place an X in that row. You'll have an opportunity to discuss your responses after you've both completed the exercise.

VALUES	PARTNER A	PARTNER B
ACCEPTANCE OF OTHERS		
BEAUTY		
COMMITMENT		
COMPASSION		
COMPETITION		
FAIRNESS		
FAITHFULNESS		
GENTLENESS		

VALUES	PARTNER A	PARTNER B
HONESTY		
INVESTMENT IN FAMILY		
KINDNESS		
PATIENCE		
POLITICAL AND SOCIAL ENGAGEMENT		
SENSITIVITY TO OTHERS' NEEDS		
SIMPLICITY OF LIFESTYLE		
SOCIAL EXCHANGE		
SPIRITUAL INVOLVEMENT		
SUCCESS		
UNWILLINGNESS TO HURT OTHERS		
ADD YOUR OWN	**PARTNER A**	**PARTNER B**

Partner Discussion

Compare your responses and discuss any that might have surprised you. Perhaps your partner chose "political and social engagement," but you are not political at all. That's okay. These are your personal values. You can each pursue avenues of interest and importance to you that don't require your partner to be on board. You can still grow together as a couple without valuing the exact same things or with the same level of intensity.

Discussion Notes

_____

_____

_____

_____

_____

Commitments to Your Morals and Values

Now that you've defined your code of conduct, you will want to explore the depth of your intentions to live up to these morals and values. Living up to what you say you will do reveals your trustworthiness to your partner. Sometimes we have blind spots that keep us from seeing what we intend to be and how we actually follow through on our commitments. Our partner can serve as our mirror to reflect back to us when we lose our way.

Agree to have open conversations when either of you notice that the other is not living up to their ideals. It's easy to get defensive around this, but the more you seek to be vulnerable and open, the more you will grow from this type of feedback.

SPIRITUALITY/RELIGION

Religion and spirituality represent one of the principal dimensions of being human. Yet we live in an age where many people seek to separate themselves from the tradition in which they grew up. As we turn to this topic, I imagine everyone comes to this workbook with a different perspective. Even if you consider yourself non-religious or not spiritually inclined, I invite you to interact with this part of the workbook together.

WHAT RESONATES FOR YOU?

Place a checkmark in the box next to any statement regarding spirituality and religion that resonates for you. Give each statement careful consideration. You'll have an opportunity to discuss your answers when you've both completed this exercise.

☐ I cultivate spirituality through practices such as prayer or scripture reading.

☐ I do not consider myself religious or spiritual, but I am on a journey to discover a way of life that makes me feel fully alive and enables me to strive toward an ethical and moral life.

☐ I have a sense of a divinity or higher power from whom I receive comfort and guidance.

☐ Meditation and mindfulness are my spiritual practices.

☐ My religion provides me with a deep family connection to a cultural way of perceiving myself in the world, which includes loyalties and a deep sense of right and wrong.

☐ Science helps us understand the world; spirituality and religion are not topics I take seriously.

☐ Spiritual involvement gives me a sense of belonging.

☐ Spirituality helps me find a sense of meaning and purpose as I shape my life through the choices I make.

☐ Spirituality is feeling guided by the teachings of my faith, giving me hope amidst the difficult times and helping me meet those times with courage.

☐ The spiritual journey encompasses anything that encourages me to think beyond myself and to care about something that matters outside my realm of self-focus.

☐ I cultivate spirituality through practices such as prayer or scripture reading.

☐ I do not consider myself religious or spiritual, but I am on a journey to discover a way of life that makes me feel fully alive and enables me to strive toward an ethical and moral life.

☐ I have a sense of divinity or higher power from whom I receive comfort and guidance.

☐ Meditation and mindfulness are my spiritual practices.

- [ ] My religion provides me with a deep family connection to a cultural way of perceiving myself in the world, which includes loyalties and a deep sense of right and wrong.
- [ ] Science helps us understand the world; spirituality and religion are not topics I take seriously.
- [ ] Spiritual involvement gives me a sense of belonging.
- [ ] Spirituality helps me find a sense of meaning and purpose as I shape my life through the choices I make.
- [ ] Spirituality is feeling guided by the teachings of my faith, giving me hope amidst the difficult times and helping me meet those times with courage.
- [ ] The spiritual journey encompasses anything that encourages me to think beyond myself and to care about something that matters outside my realm of self-focus.

Partner Discussion

While a spiritual practice is deeply personal, marriage requires you to understand and respect your partner's spiritual needs. Different responses are not a sign of incompatibility. They're a sign that you each approach spirituality differently and each approach is equally valid. Discuss ways to support each other's spiritual growth, whether or not your spiritual approaches match.

Discussion Notes

_____

_____

_____

_____

_____

IDENTIFY SIGNIFICANT INFLUENCES

Discuss the religious and spiritual influences you each had growing up. Start by naming the significant people in your life who helped shape your sense of what religion/spirituality means to you in the space provided. Then, write a brief description of what you experienced with the people who had an influence on your present choices.

> ### PARTNER A

The following people influenced my present-day choices around spirituality/religion:

_____

_____

This is what I experienced:

_____

_____

_____

_____

_____

> ### PARTNER B

The following people influenced my present-day choices around spirituality/religion:

_____

_____

This is what I experienced:

_____

_____

_____

_____

_____

Partner Discussion

Discuss your responses and ask questions of each other to dig deeper. Can you put yourself in your partner's shoes and imagine how you would have been influenced by those same people and experiences? Explore this with each other.

Discussion Notes

_____

_____

_____

_____

_____

YOUR RELIGIOUS/SPIRITUAL BACKGROUND

To understand your spiritual path so far, you'll need to look back to where it began. The following worksheet will help you identify how your religious upbringing informs your present spirituality. You can discuss your responses after the worksheet is completed:

QUESTIONS	PARTNER A	PARTNER B
WHAT RELIGION/SPIRITUAL COMMUNITY OR CULTURAL GROUP DID YOU IDENTIFY WITH AS A CHILD?		
HOW OFTEN DID YOU ATTEND RELIGIOUS SERVICES?		
DO YOU FEEL ALIENATED FROM YOUR RELIGION OR GROUP OF ORIGIN?		
DID YOUR RELIGIOUS/SPIRITUAL INVOLVEMENT GIVE YOU COMFORT AND A SENSE OF BELONGING?		

QUESTIONS	PARTNER A	PARTNER B
WERE YOUR PARENTS THE SAME RELIGION/SPIRITUAL ORIENTATION?		
DID YOU FIND SOLACE IN SPIRITUAL/RELIGIOUS EXPERIENCES APART FROM YOUR PARENTS?		
WERE YOUR PARENTS DEEPLY RELIGIOUS IN THEIR OBSERVANCES AND CELEBRATIONS?		
WERE YOUR GRANDPARENTS DEEPLY RELIGIOUS IN THEIR OBSERVANCES AND CELEBRATIONS?		
WAS ANYONE IN YOUR FAMILY A MEMBER OF THE CLERGY? IF SO, WHO?		
WERE YOUR PARENTS AND/OR GRANDPARENTS UNWELCOMING OF OTHERS OUTSIDE THEIR COMMUNITY OR FROM DIFFERENT CULTURES OR RELIGIONS?		
WERE SOCIAL CAUSES MORE IMPORTANT TO YOUR PARENTS AND/OR GRANDPARENTS THAN RELIGION/SPIRITUAL PRACTICES?		
WAS ANYONE IN YOUR FAMILY AN AVOWED ATHEIST? IF SO, WHO?		
WAS ANYONE IN YOUR FAMILY AGNOSTIC? IF SO, WHO?		
WAS ANYONE IN YOUR FAMILY CURIOUS ABOUT OTHER RELIGIONS /SPIRITUAL PRACTICES? IF SO, WHO?		

Partner Discussion

In reviewing the worksheet together, can you identify places where your paths were similar? Look for common ground, no matter how much your practices might differ based on your upbringing. Recognize that your partner's spiritual journey and that of their family is as valid as yours and your family's.

Discussion Notes

_____

_____

_____

_____

_____

BLENDING YOUR SPIRITUAL/RELIGIOUS BACKGROUNDS

Engaged couples can become overly focused on what they believe when their beliefs are not in alignment. They get into disputes about doctrines that alienate them from each other. In the case of different beliefs, looking for common ground is critical to your marriage.

Whatever your background, religious/spiritual practices encourage us to strive toward becoming better people, both for ourselves and for others. This is what you will want to strive for in your marriage, too.

Some engaged couples become less involved with their denomination or spiritual community, while others continue to faithfully attend services. If you have similar backgrounds, it's easy to pursue the offerings of your faith community together. But when you come from different worlds, you will want to explore what will work for the two of you as a couple. Consider attending each other's religious/spiritual services to discover whether either of you can feel at home there. Perhaps you can each attend the other's place of worship on special holidays. Some couples use their engagement as an opportunity to find a community that seems like a fair compromise so that each partner can identify with parts of the service.

FIND YOUR IDEAL FAITH COMMUNITY

Place a checkmark next to any statement that is true for you. You'll have a chance to discuss your responses after you've both completed the exercise:

PARTNER A

☐ I want to be part of a large religious/spiritual organization that offers many different programs throughout the year.

☐ I would enjoy meeting with a small group of people that I can get to know in depth to discuss spiritual and/or religious topics.

☐ I want to find a congregation that has discussion groups that tackle deep spiritual questions in addition to weekly services.

☐ I want to belong to a congregation whose members commit to social action.

☐ I want the place I go to worship to include the rituals that have meant something to me over the years.

☐ I would like to join a group that offers meditation and yoga.

☐ Other:

☐ Other:

▶ PARTNER B ◀

☐ I want to be part of a large religious/spiritual organization that offers many different programs throughout the year.

☐ I would enjoy meeting with a small group of people that I can get to know in depth to discuss spiritual and/or religious topics.

☐ I want to find a congregation that has discussion groups that tackle deep spiritual questions in addition to weekly services.

☐ I want to belong to a congregation whose members commit to social action.

☐ I want the place I go to worship to include the rituals that have meant something to me over the years.

☐ I would like to join a group that offers meditation and yoga.

☐ Other:

☐ Other:

Partner Discussion

Compare your checklists and identify where your needs reflect each other's. Then look for places of spiritual practice that meet those needs for both of you.

Discussion Notes

_____

_____

_____

_____

_____

MERGING TWO PATHS INTO ONE

If you come from similar backgrounds, it will likely be easy for you to continue the traditions you have both grown up with. However, if your traditions are very different, you may feel concerned that you'll be unable to find a good compromise. You'll need to take steps to support each other's journey while still being true to your own. Couples tend to work out this issue by having long and open conversations that explore what means the most to them. Here are a few solutions you may want to consider:

1. If one of you feels less passionate about their path, maybe that partner will convert to the other's religion or at least join the other in their religious observances. Even if you don't convert, in some cases you can still become a member of your partner's congregation.
2. One of you may fade away from religious observances entirely and spend time in other ways to recharge your inner batteries.
3. You both may remain loyal to your separate traditions and observe the different holidays, inviting your partner to join you when appropriate.
4. You may choose to carry out the traditions of both of your holidays and holy days and decide not to attend services at all or just on special occasions.

Regardless of your choice, be sure to stay in touch with each other on how you are finding meaning and purpose in your life. Be sure to continue growing in acceptance of your partner's journey.

YOUR CHILDREN'S MORALS AND VALUES

Children will find their spiritual/religious worldview from watching you as their role models. So, as you plan how you want your future children to grow in their faith and/or develop their morals and values, think about what traditions and rituals you want to include in their lives—especially if the two of you come from different religious backgrounds.

RITUALS IN YOUR CHILD'S LIFE

In the worksheet below, identify which traditions and rituals each of you would like your future children to participate in. Add in any traditions or rituals not included here. If the tradition or ritual is important to you, rank its importance on a scale from 1 (low) to 5 (high). If it's not important to you at all, place an X in that row. You'll have an opportunity to discuss your choices with each other after you've both completed the exercise.

TRADITION	PARTNER A	PARTNER B
BAPTISM		
BAR/BAT MITZVAH		
BRIS		
CONFIRMATION		
HOLY COMMUNION		
MEATLESS MEALS		
OBSERVANCE OF HOLY DAYS		
PRAYER BEFORE MEALS		
PRAYERS BEFORE BED		
READING HOLY SCRIPTURES		
RELIGIOUS INSTRUCTION		

TRADITION	PARTNER A	PARTNER B
SERVICE PROJECTS		
SHABBAT SERVICE AND OBSERVANCE		
WEEKLY SERVICES		
ADD YOUR OWN	**PARTNER A**	**PARTNER B**

Partner Discussion

For areas where you are not in agreement, discuss why you feel these rituals are important to your child's religious upbringing. If you experienced these moments yourself, explain what they meant to you. For those rituals you'd rather not include, calmly explain why. Look for ways you might compromise that will leave everyone feeling spiritually fulfilled.

Discussion Notes

_____

_____

_____

_____

_____

FAMILY RITUALS AND CUSTOMS

Each culture and tradition has unique rituals, traditions, and customs that may vary even among families who share a similar path. How you experienced your rituals and customs in your formative years may feel like the best way to do them going forward. Yet, in an effort to merge your traditions together, look to the richness of how your partner traditionally observes holidays and religious milestones. Be open to what your partner's traditions offer. If you can come to appreciate what these rituals and customs mean to your partner and their family, you may broaden your vision of the purpose of life.

REMEMBER MEANINGFUL RITUALS

Recall moments in your life when you felt moved by a ritual or an experience around your family's customs. Jot down some of the highlights in the space provided. After you've done this, share with each other what it means to you and how it has shaped who you are. Show appreciation for your partner's experiences, even if they are very different from your own.

> PARTNER A

_____

_____

_____

_____

_____

> PARTNER B

_____

_____

_____

_____

_____

Discussion Notes

_____

_____

_____

_____

COUPLE CHECK-IN

Flip back through this chapter and review your responses to the exercises. Were there any sticking points that one or both of you would like to revisit and work on more? What were your three biggest takeaways from this part of the workbook? Take notes in the spaces provided and discuss the items you've listed. Make an agreement to return to the exercises each of you would like to work further on before moving ahead to the next chapter.

PARTNER A

Exercises I would like to work on more:

_____

_____

_____

_____

My three biggest takeaways were:

1. _____

2. _____

3. _____

Exercises I would like to work on more:

_____

_____

_____

_____

_____

My three biggest takeaways were:

1. _____

2. _____

3. _____

ACTION ITEMS

1. Identify two rituals from a religious/spiritual path other than your own. Read about those together and discuss what it would be like to experience the richness of that culture. If you can, speak with someone from that tradition to hear their firsthand description of what those rituals mean to them.

2. Speak with married couples who follow different religious/spiritual paths to discover how they managed to merge their traditions.

3. Participate in a social event at the various congregations you are considering joining and get to know a few people.

4. Record your parents and/or grandparents talking about their culture and beliefs. This will be a special keepsake for many years to come.

5. Get a book of spiritual quotations to read from together from time to time. Choose one each, read the quote, and then talk about the meaning you each draw from it.

CHAPTER

Family and Friends

ONCE YOU'VE ANNOUNCED YOUR engagement and started to think about planning your wedding, you will start feeling magnetic pulls from family and friends. Most will celebrate your joy and shower you with their best wishes. If you announce your engagement on social media, you will gather many "thumbs ups," congratulations, and "hearts." This type of pull draws you closer together and makes you feel great. However, some family and friends may actually interfere with or influence your plans and partnership, either intentionally or unintentionally, and you may find yourselves being pulled in opposite directions. In this chapter, you'll discover ways to face the challenges of outside influences. You'll figure out how much you want to include others in your plans and in your life as a married couple.

YOUR PARENTS

Let's first examine the relationships that usually have the most impact: your connection with your parents. They may have been such an integral part of your life that you now struggle with turning to your partner for support in making decisions, or it could be quite the opposite. As you begin to plan for your future together, one or both of you may feel a little like you are betraying the role your parents have played in your lives, or you may be relieved that their role is changing. There's a lot to explore here, so let's lead off with that.

EXPLORE THE TRANSITION

For each of the statements in this worksheet, answer true or false. Some of these may be assumptions on your part with regard to how your parents will feel. Make your best guesses.

STATEMENT	PARTNER A	PARTNER B
I HAVE ALWAYS BASED MOST OF MY DECISIONS ON MY PARENTS' ADVICE AND OPINIONS.		
WHEN WE ARE MARRIED, I WILL FEEL ALIENATED FROM MY PARENTS.		
MY PARENTS WILL WANT TO MICROMANAGE EVERYTHING WE DO.		
I KNOW MY PARENTS WILL FEEL LIKE THEY ARE LOSING THEIR "BABY," AND IT BREAKS MY HEART.		
MY PARENTS WILL SUPPORT OUR PLANS AND DECISIONS.		
IF WE DO NOT HAVE OUR WEDDING CEREMONY AT MY PARENTS' PLACE OF WORSHIP, THEY WILL FEEL DISAPPOINTED OR UPSET.		
MY PARENTS ARE EXCITED TO INCLUDE YOU IN OUR FAMILY.		
MY PARENTS WILL NEED SOME TIME TO WARM UP TO HAVING YOU AS PART OF OUR FAMILY.		
MY PARENTS WILL BE DIFFICULT TO DEAL WITH FOR ANY NUMBER OF REASONS.		
OTHER:		
OTHER:		
OTHER:		

Partner Discussion

As you share these results with each other, take a long loving look at the reality of what you will be facing as you move toward marriage. Share with each other your fears and concerns regarding your relationships with each set of parents as a married couple.

Discussion Notes

_____

_____

_____

_____

_____

A PACKAGE DEAL

Each partner comes into a partnership with long-term relationships that are important to them. When you decided to get married, you agreed to a package deal, which usually includes a set of in-laws. Coach each other now about how best to deal with your parents and siblings. Start by offering a complete picture of your time with them and other family members by responding to the following:

PARTNER A

Assuming you've moved out of your childhood home, how often do your parents expect you to visit? How do you feel about this frequency? Will you want to continue seeing them more or less frequently once you're married?

_____

_____

_____

_____

What are your most outstanding memories of spending time with your parents at their home since you've moved out?

_____

_____

_____

_____

If you have siblings, do you all typically come together at the same time? What does that look like?

_____

_____

_____

_____

Does your family have traditions when extended family joins you? What does that look like?

_____

_____

_____

_____

Do you and your siblings travel to see your parents together, and will you want to continue to do this once you get married?

_____

_____

_____

_____

Does your family have a tradition to get together every weekend for a family meal or some other activity? Do you want to continue this tradition?

_____

_____

_____

_____

Assuming you've moved out of your childhood home, how often do your parents expect you to visit? How do you feel about this frequency? Will you want to continue seeing them more or less frequently once you're married?

_____

_____

_____

_____

What are your most outstanding memories of spending time with your parents at their home since you've moved out?

_____

_____

_____

_____

If you have siblings, do you all typically come together at the same time? What does that look like?

_____

_____

_____

_____

Does your family have traditions when extended family joins you? What does that look like?

_____

_____

_____

_____

Do you and your siblings travel to see your parents together and will you want to continue to do this once you get married?

_____

_____

_____

_____

Does your family have a tradition to get together every weekend for a family meal or some other activity? Do you want to continue this tradition?

_____

_____

_____

_____

Partner Discussion

Review your responses together and have an open-minded discussion. For example, what if Sunday dinner is a tradition at both your childhood homes? What happens when each set of your parents expects you to join them for Thanksgiving dinner? Naturally, you are only beginning to think about these issues. Sometimes these issues can be quickly resolved and sometimes they will require some brainstorming to figure out a win-win for everyone. By addressing the "what ifs?" and "what will we do?" as soon as possible, you are clarifying any boundaries you need to set around your parents and in-laws.

Discussion Notes

_____

_____

_____

_____

7 TIPS FOR A ESTABLISHING A UNITED FRONT

1. Thoroughly acquaint your partner with the traditions that exist around time spent with your family, as you did in the exercise on page 145.

2. Imagine how a year of activities involving both sets of parents might look and share these thoughts with each other.

3. Decide which issues and topics you will support each other on in front of your respective families.

4. Agree to listen with an open mind to why certain things mean so much to your parents and in-laws. If they feel that you and your partner are listening to them and taking them seriously, they may eventually acquiesce; they have no real power unless you give it to them.

5. If you go against your parents' or in-laws' expectations, don't expect them to like it or accept it. You need to do what works for you as a couple since you are committing your lives to each other.

6. Discuss with each other how best to interact with your respective parents until your partner is comfortable with them. (See the exercise on page 152.)

7. Decide what type of information you will not share with your parents. For example, your parents do not need to know about your sex life, just as you don't need to know anything about theirs. You may choose to keep details regarding your finances to yourselves, and you may choose to keep details of any disagreements private. If they ask, maintain your united front and say, "We agreed to keep that between us."

BEHAVIOR AROUND PARENTS

You each grew up relating to your parents in a certain way. Part of the dilemma in dealing with in-laws stems from how you learned to interact with your own parents. The easiest way to interact with your parents might include a pattern of behavior that seems strange to your partner. For instance, your partner may keep their feelings private around their parents because they felt belittled when they expressed certain emotions growing up, while you shared everything with your parents. Use the following prompts to share with your partner what you have noticed about their behavior around their parents. You'll have a chance to discuss why you learned to behave in certain ways after you've both completed this exercise.

> **PARTNER A**

When you are around your parents, I notice that you:

_____

_____

_____

_____

_____

When you do this, I feel:

_____

_____

_____

_____

_____

Is it possible that next time we are with your parents, you could:

_____

_____

_____

_____

_____

When you are around your parents, I notice that you:

_____

_____

_____

_____

_____

When you do this, I feel:

_____

_____

_____

_____

_____

Is it possible that next time we are with your parents, you could:

_____

_____

_____

_____

_____

Partner Discussion

Understand that everyone's experiences with their parents are unique. Many people act a certain way around their parents not only to protect themselves, but also to protect their partners. Ask your partner what drives their motives for acting the way they do, and discuss your concerns with compassion. That said, be honest when you feel a certain behavior is problematic for you as you deal with parents and in-laws.

Discussion Notes

_____

_____

_____

_____

_____

WHAT WOULD YOUR PARENTS APPRECIATE?

Here's an opportunity to come up with ideas to help your partner identify ways to earn your parents' respect. You probably know your parents quite well, so help your partner out here. You may also want to steer your partner away from pushing your parents' hot buttons. Check all the items that apply. You'll have a chance to discuss your suggestions with each other after you've each had a chance to respond.

▶ PARTNER A ◀

These are some ways I think you can earn my parents' respect:

- ☐ Show up on time for gatherings
- ☐ Give them thoughtful gifts
- ☐ Write them thank-you notes
- ☐ Watch sports with them
- ☐ Prepare a meal with them
- ☐ Offer them sincere compliments

8 TIPS FOR FINDING ACCEPTANCE AROUND YOUR IN-LAWS

Part of marrying your partner includes finding a way to have the best possible relationship you can have with your in-laws. It comes with the territory. Try to find peace with the reality of who your partner's parents are. As tempting as it might be, avoid setting up any situation where your partner has to choose between you and their parents.

Here are eight tips to help you each find acceptance around the sometimes touchy subject of in-laws:

1. Acknowledge that these people will always be your partner's parents and need to be treated with the same respect you show to others.

2. Agree with your partner that you have a right to share how it feels to be around your in-laws. When you share your feelings, try not to attack your in-laws' character or have their flaws reflect on your partner. In return, listen to your partner's experience and validate the feelings they share.

3. Learn how to identify when something isn't a big deal and let it slide.

4. Avoid making dismissive comments about your partner's parents in regular conversation to other people and to your partner.

5. If your partner's complaints about your parents seem unfair, try to hear them out anyway. Whenever you can, validate their feelings by putting yourself in their shoes. If their parents had done the same to you, how would you feel?

6. Don't allow your in-laws to divide and conquer you. Find a solution you can stand behind as a couple.

7. Always keep in mind that your in-laws did their best to provide for and care for your partner, even if it was less than ideal.

8. Identify things about your partner that you love and admire, and see if you can recognize that your in-laws helped your partner develop those qualities.

☐ Ask questions about how they met
☐ Talk about politics and the news—or not!
☐ Play a game with them
☐ Plan a trip with them
☐ Join them for family dinners
☐ Discuss topics of interest with them
☐ Tell them about yourself
☐ _____
☐ _____
☐ _____
☐ _____

These are some ways I think you can earn my parents' respect:

☐ Show up on time for gatherings
☐ Give them thoughtful gifts
☐ Write them thank-you notes
☐ Watch sports with them
☐ Prepare a meal with them
☐ Offer them sincere compliments
☐ Ask questions about how they met
☐ Talk about politics and the news—or not!
☐ Play a game with them
☐ Plan a trip with them
☐ Join them for family dinners
☐ Discuss topics of interest with them
☐ Tell them about yourself
☐ _____
☐ _____
☐ _____
☐ _____

Partner Discussion

As you review your answers, consider what might make you feel more comfortable about trying these ideas out. If there are any suggestions that don't sit well with you, tell your partner why. Also discuss how it would feel to honor your partner's requests. Identify how you expect honoring those requests will affect your relationship with your partner and with your partner's parents.

Discussion Notes

_____

_____

_____

_____

_____

You may squirm when your partner says or does something around your parents that you would never say or do—or at least that you don't feel is appropriate for your partner to say or do. Have a conversation to bring this issue into the light and suggest a different approach in the future. Here's an example of a productive conversation:

Partner A: "When you talk to my parents about money, I feel uneasy. Knowing my parents, they will want to swoop in and rescue us or feel like we're not working hard enough."

Partner B: "Let me see if I got you. You feel uneasy when I bring up money issues with your parents because they will want to give us money or judge us for not earning enough. I can appreciate you might feel that way. We work hard to bring in what we need, and you have always wanted to be independent of them."

Partner A: "That's true. I would be comfortable in the future if we only talk in general terms about money without being specific about our finances. Would that work for you?"

Partner B: "Yes, I won't disclose any of our private financial matters with your parents."

Now it's your turn. Pick something your partner does around your parents that you would prefer they stop doing and fill in the blanks:

When you _____ with my parents,

I start feeling _____. As a result,

I suspect my parents might _____.

This concerns me because _____.

I would appreciate it if you would instead _____.

Would that work for you?

When you _____ with my parents,

I start feeling _____. As a result,

I suspect my parents might _____.

This concerns me because _____.

I would appreciate it if you would instead _____.

Would that work for you?

Partner Discussion

You might get defensive when your partner asks you to adjust your behavior. If you find yourself feeling this way, remember that your partner's intention is not to hurt, change, or chastise you. Your partner's intention is to improve your relationship both with their parents and between the two of you. Positive growth is the goal here. When you get married, you promise to protect and nurture your marriage, and sometimes that means restraining yourself from doing or saying things to your partner's parents that might hurt their feelings or invite them to interfere with your marriage. Brainstorm ways to focus on the goal of nurturing your marriage during in-law conflict.

Discussion Notes

_____

_____

_____

_____

_____

"FORSAKING ALL OTHERS"

Consider the familiar wording of traditional marriage ceremonies: Mixed in with the requested promises of loving, comforting, honoring, and keeping your partner, so long as you both shall live, often comes the request to forsake all others in favor of your spouse. But what does it mean to forsake all others?

The promise to forsake all others is separate from the promise to be faithful to your spouse because it addresses a totally different aspect of your marriage. Forsaking all others means turning to one another first, considering the other's feelings, concerns, and ideas before running to others—including one's parents—for solutions, advice, or approval.

This does not mean that you cannot continue to get support and insight from your parents. It simply means that you do not let your loyalty to them come between you and your partner.

WHAT DOES THIS MEAN TO YOU?

This exercise helps you explore what "forsaking" means for each of you, both as a means of self-exploration and as a means of setting expectations of yourself and your partner for the future. Visualize the moment in your wedding ceremony where you will turn to face one another.

How will it feel to place your hand in the hand of your partner to be joined in marriage? Describe how you think that moment will feel for you:

> PARTNER A

_____

_____

_____

With this moment in mind, imagine the question of forsaking arises. Knowing you will be joining yourself to your partner and knowing part of that promise includes "forsake all others," consider what forsaking looks like for you.

How much are you willing to forsake all others, no matter who they are, in favor of building a supportive, loving, lifelong relationship with your partner? How much do you expect them to do the same?

PARTNER A

_____

_____

_____

PARTNER B

_____

_____

_____

Partner Discussion

Do your individual answers to these questions reflect the other's expectations? Discuss whether or not you feel that forsaking all others will be easy or difficult, particularly in interactions with your parents. Agree to revisit this exercise and ask yourselves if you are keeping your promise to forsake all others.

_____

_____

_____

_____

_____

SIBLINGS

Your brothers and sisters have known you all their lives. Now that you're getting married, they may feel as if you are abandoning them and feeling like your sibling bond will be weakened. Have open discussions with your siblings to let them know how much they mean to you. Many of the discussions and exercises you've done in this chapter around your parents can also be applied toward your siblings, especially if one or more of them had a parental role in your life growing up. With that in mind, let's take a different tack here.

In my premarital counseling inventory, I always ask couples if their partners remind them of any of their siblings. While it's true that sometimes we choose our partners because they remind us of our parents, we might also choose someone who reminds us of one of our brothers or sisters. Here's why: We are usually comfortable around our siblings because we spent so many years learning how to get along with them. When we meet someone who reminds us of them, we naturally feel drawn to them because a certain level of comfort already exists.

As you can imagine, this has its strengths and weaknesses. Because not every sibling relationship is perfect, if you subconsciously chose your partner for this reason, you might find yourself replaying old issues or arguments you had with that sibling with your partner instead. This is something you'll want to learn how to avoid.

IDENTIFY SIMILARITIES AND DIFFERENCES

Think about your partner's characteristics and compare them to each of your siblings. Figure out which one your partner is most like, and respond to the following:

▶ PARTNER A ◀

What similarities do your partner and sibling share?

_____

_____

_____

Recall a situation when being with your partner felt similar to when you are with that sibling, and describe it:

_____

_____

_____

In what ways is your partner entirely different from your sibling?

_____

_____

_____

▶ PARTNER B ◀

What similarities do your partner and sibling share?

_____

_____

_____

Recall a situation when being with your partner felt similar to when you are with that sibling, and describe it:

_____

_____

_____

In what ways is your partner entirely different from your sibling?

_____

_____

_____

Partner Discussion

Discuss your responses and tell each other stories about your interactions with the sibling you identified. Place focus on the differences between your sibling and partner to remind the "computer" in your mind that this is a different person. If you find yourself falling into old patterns, like arguments and behaviors, that were common with that sibling, agree to be conscious of times when you approach your partner with anger left over from interactions with your sibling.

Discussion Notes

_____

_____

_____

_____

_____

FAMILY HOLIDAYS, VISITS, AND VACATION

Like many couples, you may find getting together with both families for special occasions a bit of a challenge to work out. You may be able to figure out a fair exchange by alternating holidays each year. However, some families may not be able to conceive of spending some part of important holidays without you. Some families deal with this by having everyone meet at a central place, which is a nice idea, but it can become complicated when siblings and their partners' families are also involved.

Resolving these issues comes with the territory of becoming a couple. You will probably not be able to make everyone happy with the decisions you arrive at as a couple. You may even discover that you want to spend time alone as a couple when you used to spend time with family. Fortunately, throughout this workbook, you've been practicing the fine art of finding win-win solutions. This happens when you share your past experiences and feelings and try to understand where your partner is coming from.

This exercise helps you share with your partner what you have in mind moving forward with regard to holidays, family visits, and vacations. Remember, right now you are sharing your preferences and letting your partner know why they are important to you. Start by answering the first set of questions as a couple:

We plan to observe the following holidays:

_____

_____

_____

_____

_____

We plan to take _____ vacations each year.

If we must travel to see family, we will try to do this _____ times each year.

PARTNER A

I would like to share the following holidays with my family:

_____

_____

_____

This is important to me because:

_____

_____

_____

_____

_____

I would like to spend our vacations together this way:

_____

_____

_____

_____

This is how I envision spending time with my family:

_____

_____

_____

My family may feel hurt if we do not:

_____

_____

_____

> PARTNER B <

I would like to share the following holidays with my family:

_____

_____

_____

This is important to me because:

_____

_____

_____

_____

_____

I would like to spend our vacations together this way:

_____

_____

_____

_____

_____

This is how I envision spending time with my family:

_____

_____

_____

My family may feel hurt if we do not:

_____

_____

_____

Part Discussion

Now that you've both laid your cards on the table, see where your wishes conflict. If you can't easily come up with a solution, it's time to compromise. Brainstorm ways you can each get your desire to spend time with your families met while honoring that you're all family now. There's really no mine or yours once you get married.

Discussion Notes

_____

_____

_____

_____

THE MATTER OF AGING PARENTS

It may be a long way off, but start discussing now what your feelings are around elder care once your parents become unable to care for themselves. Perhaps your parents have already made arrangements for their old age and have adequate insurance to cover full-time care if and when the need arises. This isn't the reality for most people though, so if your parents haven't discussed their long-term care plan with you, ask them if they feel comfortable doing so. In the meantime, be sure that you and your partner are on the same page with the eventuality that one or more of your parents may need your assistance.

THOUGHTS ON ELDER CARE

Respond to the following prompts as honestly as possible. You don't have to answer what you believe is the correct answer but what you truly feel is best for you as a couple.

> PARTNER A <

If one of your elderly parents or in-laws required support, in what way do you imagine offering them that support, if at all?

_____

_____

Would you feel comfortable inviting an elderly parent to live in your home?

_____

_____

Do you have the financial resources to help an elderly parent if necessary?

_____

_____

Do you have siblings who will pitch in to help?

_____

_____

_____

Do you feel comfortable with the idea of your parents being in a nursing home or an assisted-living facility?

_____

_____

_____

If one of your elderly parents or in-laws required support, in what way do you imagine offering them that support, if at all?

_____

_____

_____

Would you feel comfortable inviting an elderly parent to live in your home?

_____

_____

_____

Do you have the financial resources to help an elderly parent if necessary?

_____

_____

_____

Do you have siblings who will pitch in to help?

_____

_____

_____

Do you feel comfortable with the idea of your parents being in a nursing home or an assisted-living facility?

_____

_____

_____

Partner Discussion

Where do your expectations align and where do they differ? Approach this conversation with as much compassion as you can. You each may feel the need to take care of your parents in their old age. As this is likely a long time from now, consider how your relationships will grow with your respective in-laws. If you can't fathom having an in-law living with you someday, realize that as time goes by, you might actually come to a point when they are just as important to you as your own parents are.

Discussion Notes

_____

_____

_____

_____

_____

FRIENDSHIPS

Your friends can be an amazing source of fun and support as you go through the transition from engaged to married. It's also true that some of your friends might make the transition from single to married harder on you.

You might each be attached to the circle of friends you hung out with before you met your partner. If you share a circle of friends, great! You can all still hang out together occasionally. But if you each had different friend groups and your friends don't mesh or, worse yet, your friends don't like your choice of partner, you may notice power struggles, hurt feelings, jealousy, or other reactions that come up when people feel like they're losing someone important to them. Your friends may also resent the fact that you are spending less time with them now that you are engaged.

Have compassion but also realize that you have made your choice with who you want to spend your life with. If your friends can't support that or are critical of your partner, you will need to distance yourself and possibly break off the friendship for the future of your relationship.

IDENTIFY SUPPORTIVE FRIENDS

In this worksheet, make a list of *all* of your friends—mine, yours, and ours. List married or engaged couples together. Be sure to include anyone and everyone you consider a friend. If you think this friend or couple supports you and will be a cheerleader for you as you move into married life, write "yes" in the space provided. If not, write "no." You may even say "maybe." You'll have an opportunity to discuss your responses after you've both completed this worksheet.

FRIENDS/COUPLES	PARTNER A	PARTNER B

Partner Discussion

Expect that sometimes you will not agree on whether your friendships are helpful or harmful to your marriage, particularly in the case of lifelong friends. If either of you notices that your partner treats you differently after they've spent time with certain friends, be willing to explore this together. Acknowledge your partner's concerns and be willing to discuss your options. Also recognize that, even in the case of toxic friendships, it may be difficult for you or your partner to end friendships that can harm your marriage. Be compassionate and as supportive as possible of each other if you find yourselves having to cut old friends out of your married life.

Discussion Notes

_____

_____

_____

_____

_____

SCHEDULE TIME FOR FRIENDS

How much time do each of you want to devote to getting together with friends? Just because you've always spent Saturday nights with your friends doesn't mean you will continue do to this when you start building your married life together. Think about the time you have with your partner, taking into consideration the time you spend with family and on your careers. Also, take into account if you're the type who prefers to spend quiet time curled up on the couch while your partner loves to be with people.

In this worksheet, identify your ideal number of times a month you'd like to spend with friends.

	NUMBER OF TIMES PER MONTH I'D LIKE TO SPEND WITH MY FRIENDS ON MY OWN	NUMBER OF TIMES PER MONTH I'D LIKE TO SPEND WITH OUR FRIENDS AS A COUPLE	NUMBER OF TIMES PER MONTH I'D LIKE TO ATTEND PARTIES OR GET-TOGETHERS
PARTNER A			
PARTNER B			

Partner Discussion

Are your thoughts here in alignment? Take this a step further and identify how much time you're talking about. Do you want to go out to dinner with your friends on your own once or twice a month? Will you be gone for two, three, maybe four hours? Do you want to watch the game over at your friend's house every Sunday? How much time are you talking about? Discuss how each of you feels about the time apart. Also discuss the time you spend with other couples and at parties. Figure out what works for both of you and identify compromises to arrive at the win-win. For example, can you have a dinner out with your favorite couple but come home to cuddle on the couch afterward?

Discussion Notes

_____

_____

_____

_____

_____

COUPLE CHECK-IN

Flip back through this chapter and review your responses to the exercises. Were there any sticking points that one or both of you would like to revisit and work on more? What were your three biggest takeaways from this part of the workbook? Take notes in the spaces provided and discuss the items you've listed. Make an agreement to return to the exercises you would like to work further on before moving ahead to the next chapter.

Exercises I would like to work on more:

_____

_____

_____

_____

_____

My three biggest takeaways were:

1. _____

2. _____

3. _____

Exercises I would like to work on more:

_____

_____

_____

_____

_____

My three biggest takeaways were:

1. _____

2. _____

3. _____

ACTIONS ITEMS

1. Ask your married friends how they worked out some of the common issues with their in-laws and parents. While they may have standard complaints, press for how they've managed to deal with the

disagreements and disappointments, even if it just meant distancing themselves.

2. Watch a movie that portrays the interactions between engaged/married couples with their in-laws. After the movie, have a conversation about what occurred in the movie to bring the couple closer together.

3. Role-play what you might think will happen at an upcoming family gathering and figure out ways to present a united front despite what's going on or other people's reactions.

4. Think of a fun way to bond with your partner's friends and plan something your partner thinks they will like.

5. Have your ancestry tested through a service like 23andMe.com or Ancestry.com to discover what your DNA says about your family tree. Compare your results and share it with your families as interesting conversation starters.

CHAPTER

8

Work

WORK GIVES MEANING TO our lives and offers us a means to support ourselves. It's often been said that people spend at least one-third of their life working and one-third of their life sleeping. So, naturally, your happiness at work is a principal source of satisfaction in life. Having a fulfilling job improves and enhances the attitude you bring home to your relationship at the end of the day.

When people love their work, it becomes their passion. When they don't, it can become a significant source of stress. Couples who share the highs and lows of their experiences at work find that it brings them closer. That mutual catching up with each other after work can cushion the impact of a stressful day or allow you to celebrate your or your partner's success.

In this chapter, you will explore your attitudes toward work, your workload, and how you plan to divide the chores at home. Figuring this out before you get back from your honeymoon gives you an idea of what to expect going forward.

CAREER EXPECTATIONS

Naturally, you have aspirations when it comes to your careers. These aspirations can serve as a source of feeling in sync or as an arena for dissatisfaction. Finding meaning in your career will contribute to the satisfaction in your marriage, so the more you appreciate each other's vision, the more you can support each other and bond around it. Expectations include factors like:

- The time each of you will spend at work (or whether only one of you will work).
- The salary each of you plans to make to support yourselves and your children, if you decide to have them.
- How much your work life spills over into your home life (e.g., after dinner and/or on weekends).
- Whether one or both of you will continue your education.
- Whether one or both of you will need to work two jobs.
- Whether entertaining business associates is a part of your job.

All of these expectations will be fully explored in the exercises and discussions to follow. As with everything you've done so far, it's best to start at the beginning: what you learned from your parents.

YOUR PARENTS' WORK-LIFE BALANCE

What did you learn from your parents about work-life balance when you were growing up? Maybe your parents worked so hard to make ends meet that you never really got to spend any quality time with them. Or maybe only one parent worked and the other was available 24/7. Perhaps your parents were able to support the family through hard work but they also made room to spend time with you doing fun things. You may feel drawn to your parents' model or compelled to approach your work-life balance differently.

To figure out where each of you stand, start by examining your parents' approach by writing "true," "false," or "sometimes" for each of the statements listed in this worksheet.

PARENTS' WORK-LIFE BALANCE	PARTNER A	PARTNER B
BOTH OF MY PARENTS WORKED WHILE I WAS GROWING UP.		
ONE OF MY PARENTS CARRIED THE LOAD BECAUSE THE OTHER WASN'T AROUND.		
I HAD A STAY-AT-HOME PARENT WHO TOOK CARE OF THE HOME AND CHILDREN.		
THE STAY-AT-HOME PARENT WENT BACK TO WORK AFTER WE CHILDREN GREW UP.		
ONLY ONE OF MY PARENTS BROUGHT IN A SALARY BUT THE OTHER DID A LOT OF VOLUNTEER WORK.		
MY PARENTS SEEMED SATISFIED WITH THEIR WORK-LIFE BALANCE.		
MY PARENTS SEEMED DISSATISFIED WITH THEIR WORK-LIFE BALANCE.		
ONE PARENT WORKED MUCH HARDER THAN THE OTHER, AND THIS WAS A SOURCE OF ARGUMENTS IN OUR HOME.		
IT SEEMED LIKE ONE OR BOTH OF MY PARENTS WERE WORKING ALL THE TIME JUST TO SUPPORT US.		
ONE PARENT WORKED PART TIME AND THE OTHER WORKED FULL TIME.		
MY PARENTS WORKED IN THE EVENINGS AND/OR ON THE WEEKENDS.		
ONE OR BOTH OF MY PARENTS WORKED FROM HOME.		
MY PARENTS HAD FLEXIBLE SCHEDULES SO THEY WERE ALWAYS ABLE TO ATTEND SCHOOL FUNCTIONS TOGETHER.		
BUSINESS CALLS WOULD OFTEN INTERRUPT FAMILY TIME.		
ONE OF MY PARENTS HAD TO TRAVEL FOR WORK AND WAS OFTEN AWAY ON BUSINESS TRIPS.		
MY PARENTS BUILT A BUSINESS TOGETHER AND WORKED SIDE BY SIDE.		
ONE OF MY PARENTS GOT HOME VERY LATE FROM WORK NEARLY EVERY DAY.		
BOTH OF MY PARENTS LOVED THE WORK THEY DID.		
ONE OF MY PARENTS ALWAYS COMPLAINED ABOUT THEIR JOB.		
OTHER:		
OTHER:		

Partner Discussion

Compare your responses to your parents' work-life model. Did any of your answers line up? How did they differ? How might your respective parents' approaches shape what you expect of each other and yourselves?

Discussion Notes

_____

_____

_____

_____

_____

WILL ONE OR BOTH OF YOU HAVE A CAREER?

Chances are you have already considered this question, but if not, now is a good time. Do you both need to work to sustain the lifestyle you're accustomed to or the one you envision for your future together? What scenario will work best for you when you consider your choice of neighborhood and the comforts you hope to have? Review the budget you came up with on page 57. Maybe a financial planner helped you arrive at an ideal anticipated income to remain within your budget and have some money left over for extras. Will your anticipated income suffice? These are all important questions. Begin now by identifying your preferences around what part you will play in bringing in the income you need in the following exercise.

PREFERENCES AROUND WORK-LIFE BALANCE

To figure out where each of you stands, write "true" or "false" for each of the statements listed in this worksheet. You'll have a chance to discuss your preferences after you've both completed the worksheet.

	PARTNER A	PARTNER B
I AM WILLING TO WORK 40 OR MORE HOURS AT MY JOB EACH WEEK.		
I WILL WORK OVERTIME WHEN I AM OFFERED IT OR REQUEST IT IF WE NEED THE MONEY.		
I AM WILLING TO TAKE A SECOND JOB TO HELP US MAKE ENDS MEET.		
I WANT TO WORK PART TIME.		
I PREFER TO DO VOLUNTEER WORK RATHER THAN PAID WORK.		
I WANT TO BE A STAY-AT-HOME PARENT WHEN OUR CHILDREN ARE YOUNG.		
I AM WILLING TO CUT BACK ON OUR EXPENSES SO WE DON'T HAVE TO WORK SO HARD.		
I NEED TO SPEND TIME OUTSIDE THE HOME ENTERTAINING BUSINESS ASSOCIATES AND/OR NETWORKING.		
I WANT A REGULAR NINE-TO-FIVE JOB SO I CAN ENJOY EVENINGS AND WEEKENDS RELAXING OR HAVING FUN.		
I WANT TO CONTINUE MY EDUCATION WHILE YOU WORK, AND THEN WE CAN SWITCH PLACES LATER.		
I AM WILLING TO WORK ON WEEKENDS AND IN THE EVENINGS.		
MY SALARY IS SUFFICIENT TO COVER ALL OF OUR NEEDS.		
WE NEED A COMBINED SALARY TO COVER ALL OF OUR NEEDS.		
WE WILL HAVE TO TAKE OUT A LOAN FROM THE BANK OR BORROW FROM OUR PARENTS TO GET US ON OUR FEET.		

Partner Discussion

Review your answers and identify any expectations that seem to conflict. You may find that even though you may be willing or unwilling to do certain things now, such as working on the weekends, life may play out in such a way that you will weigh all the options and end up doing what you said you would never do. Be open-minded about the future while establishing how you currently feel.

Discussion Notes

_____

_____

_____

_____

_____

DIFFERENCE IN INCOMES

If both of you are working, there's a chance one of you will bring in a higher salary than the other. This can cause a myriad of feelings. The partner who is making less may feel that they are not doing their fair share, and the partner who is making more may feel like the burden is on them to create or maintain the desired lifestyle. Keep in mind that some professions are higher paying than others, but this doesn't necessarily mean one's work is more important than another's. For example, a teacher might make less than a bank executive, but both of these professions are serving others in different but important ways.

Try to celebrate each other's contribution and look at your combined income as "ours" rather than as "mine" and "yours." For now, bring to light any feelings you have about the difference in income to help you begin to resolve or mitigate negative or uncomfortable emotions that may arise.

IDENTIFY FEELINGS AROUND THE DIFFERENCE

Take a few moments to sit together and tune in to your feelings around your salaries or your anticipated salaries (or lack of salary). Respond as fully to the following questions as you can:

> PARTNER A

If I make a larger income than you, I will probably feel (or do feel):

_____

_____

If you make a larger income than I do, I will probably feel (or do feel):

_____

_____

If you work but I don't, I will probably feel (or do feel):

_____

_____

If I work but you don't, I will probably feel (or do feel):

_____

_____

If I make a larger income than you, I will probably feel (or do feel):

_____

_____

If you make a larger income than I do, I will probably feel (or do feel):

_____

_____

If you work but I don't, I will probably feel (or do feel):

_____

_____

If I work but you don't, I will probably feel (or do feel):

_____

_____

Partner Discussion

Validate your partner's feelings with statements like, "I can understand why you would feel [fill in the blank] if I [fill in the blank] and you [fill in the blank]. Let me describe how I see it." If you can mitigate your partner's concerns, try to do that now. Do any of your partner's responses concern you? If so, discuss these concerns and see if you can each come to a place of acceptance without either one of you feeling superior or inferior.

_____

_____

_____

_____

_____

CAREER OBJECTIVES

As I mentioned earlier, work gives meaning to life *and* provides the financial means to support your lifestyle. You may each be very devoted to your current career or projected career path. However, the time you devote to your career may shift and transform as your life changes, such as with the advent of children.

You may be entering into marriage with loads of anticipation of how you will manage your work-life balance together. Continue to tease out what each of you looks forward to in creating the means to support your lifestyle. This will provide you with the opportunity to build a sense of cooperation where you work together as a team. Support each other so that you can each find satisfaction in the work you do and the reason you are doing it.

RATE YOUR CURRENT LEVEL OF SATISFACTION

On the following continuum, mark your degree of satisfaction doing the work you presently do (this may include the work you do at school or at home, too).

PARTNER A

Dissatisfied   Very Satisfied

Dissatisfied   Very Satisfied

●   ●   ●   ●   ●   ●   ●   ●   ●   ●   ●

Partner Discussion

If you are both very satisfied, go out and celebrate! However, one or both of you may fall elsewhere, perhaps even closer to dissatisfied. Brainstorm ways to support each other in finding work that is more satisfying or how to find more satisfaction where you currently are.

Discussion Notes

_____

_____

_____

_____

_____

IDENTIFY THE INGREDIENTS IN JOB SATISFACTION

This worksheet includes a list of needs around job satisfaction with room to add a few of your own. Each partner will have an opportunity to identify whether or not a particular need is important to them personally. If the need is important to you to find satisfaction in the work you do, rank its importance on a scale from 1 (low) to 5 (high). If it's not important to you at all, place an X in that row. You'll have an opportunity to discuss these needs with each other after you've both completed the exercise.

NEED	PARTNER A	PARTNER B
JOB SECURITY		
OPPORTUNITIES FOR ADVANCEMENT		
CHANCE TO TRAVEL		
FUTURE INCOME		
OFFERS PRESTIGE		
WORKING WITH A TEAM		
PLEASANT COLLEAGUES		
BEING SELF-EMPLOYED		
HOME IN EVENINGS FOR DINNER		
FLEXIBILITY TO BE WITH THE CHILDREN DURING THE DAY		
PAID HOLIDAYS AND VACATION TIME		
HEALTH PLAN		
PENSION PROGRAM		
SHORT COMMUTE		
OPPORTUNITY FOR EARLY RETIREMENT		
LIVING IN A PARTICULAR REGION OF COUNTRY		
ADD YOUR OWN	PARTNER A	PARTNER B

Partner Discussion

Different people have different needs, even when it comes to finding satisfaction in work. If you and your partner identify any needs that aren't getting met, discuss ways you can try to make that happen. For example, did one of you choose "short commute"? You can support that partner in finding work closer to home.

_____

_____

_____

_____

_____

IDENTIFYING YOUR IDEAL WORK

You may have discovered by now that you have very different attitudes toward work. Maybe you don't expect your job to give you a sense of fulfillment; it's just a means of making a living so that you can enjoy the rest of your life when you're off. On the other hand, you may feel a yearning to do something special. You want to enjoy your time off knowing you've made a difference in the lives of people who need your services. Or maybe you both want the same thing. Explore now whether or not you are in an ideal position, headed for one, or if this is still something you need to figure out.

EXPLORE YOUR THOUGHTS AROUND YOUR JOB

These writing prompts will help you gain clarity around how you feel about your current job, if you have one. If you don't have a job, skip to the last writing prompt, but support your partner with this exercise. If you do volunteer work instead of paid work, complete all of the prompts. With a little creativity, you can substitute school for work if you are still pursuing your education. You'll have a chance to compare notes after you've both completed this exercise.

5 STEPS TO RESOLVE WORK-LIFE CONFLICTS

Celebrate where your work-life expectations seem to mesh easily. If there are areas of conflict, ask your partner what makes them feel so strongly about an ideal or expectation. You may fear that your issues will have no resolution, but do not lose heart. Put in the time to look for a workable solution with the understanding that you may have to compromise. Follow these steps for coming to a win-win solution around work-life balance:

1. Identify the needs you are filling with regard to your chosen career or career expectations, as you did in the exercise on page 184.
2. Use the decision-making protocol you learned in chapter 2 to brainstorm as many options as you can to arrive at a plan for work-life balance that works for both of you.
3. While you are brainstorming, have fun and think way outside of the box by looking at your situation as if you were extraterrestrial beings making an equitable choice for a human couple.
4. Discern which solutions come the closest to what will work for each of you as lifelong partners.
5. Agree to reevaluate your decisions as time passes, recognizing that what you decide now may change as your life together evolves.

> **PARTNER A**

How happy or unhappy are you at your current job? What don't you like about it? What do you like about it?

_____

_____

_____

Did you fall into this job or did you actively pursue it?

_____

What did you do to prepare for or to find this job?

_____

_____

_____

What does this job mean to you?

_____

_____

_____

Do you see yourself in this job forever or is it a stepping-stone?

_____

Do you need more training or schooling to grow in this job?

_____

Do you anticipate being transferred to a different location by management?

_____

What are some careers you might like to pursue?

_____

How happy or unhappy are you at your current job? What don't you like about it?
What do you like about it?

_____

_____

_____

Did you fall into this job or did you actively pursue it?

_____

What did you do to prepare for this or to find this job?

_____

_____

_____

What does this job mean to you?

_____

_____

_____

Do you see yourself in this job forever or is it a stepping-stone?

_____

Do you need more training or schooling to grow in this job?

_____

Do you anticipate being transferred to a different location by management?

_____

What are some careers you might like to pursue?

_____

Partner Discussion

By sharing this history and some of your aspirations, are you getting a clearer picture of what each of you is bringing into your mutual work-life situation? Do any of your partner's responses concern you? How does your partner's feelings around their present job affect you?

Discussion Notes

_____

_____

_____

_____

WHOSE CAREER TAKES PRECEDENCE?

Back in the day, it wasn't uncommon for the wife to put her professional aspirations aside to stay home for the kids. Maybe you have already decided that one of you will stay home, and that's fine if it works for both of you. But more often than not these days, both partners work and both partners consider their careers equally important. However, if a time comes when one partner's career needs to be placed ahead of the other's, conflict may arise, causing hurt feelings and heated arguments.

If there is a transfer in the works or if one of you gets a dream job in another state and you have no intention of having a cross-continental marriage, you may be faced with a difficult choice. If you move for one partner's job, the other partner will need to find suitable employment in the new location. If you don't move, that job in another state becomes unattainable. Discussions of this nature can become heated. The more intense the discussion, the more likely you will slip into black-and-white extremes. Head this off at the pass by discussing now what you will do if there's ever a question about whose job comes first.

EXPLORE FUNDAMENTAL QUESTIONS

The following writing prompts are intended to help your partner understand the importance of your job in the event that one career must take precedence. Present your feelings by answering as honestly as you can.

> PARTNER A

How does your career path or ideal job align with the future you want to build?

_____

_____

_____

If you do not pursue this career path or have an opportunity to work in your ideal job, what part of you will you be sacrificing?

_____

_____

_____

How does your career path or ideal job align with the future you want to build?

_____

_____

_____

If you do not pursue this career path or have an opportunity to work in your ideal job, what part of you will you be sacrificing?

_____

_____

_____

Partner Discussion

Take turns sharing your answers with each other, allowing an opportunity to ask questions that will lead to a deeper understanding. Ask, for instance, "How strongly do you feel about this?" and "What other paths have you considered?" Use the answers to help determine whose career will take precedence.

Discussion Notes

_____

_____

_____

_____

Perhaps one of you has an opportunity to accept a job that will interfere with the other's ability to pursue their career or stay in a job they like. Maybe you haven't encountered this problem yet and maybe you never will. Because we can never know what the future holds, do this exercise anyway. Come up with a scenario that could potentially arise. There's no need to write down your answers here. Instead, take these steps and jot down your takeaways at the end of the prompts.

1. The first partner makes a compelling case for what accepting this opportunity means to them and why, while the other partner listens without interruption.

2. Consider as a couple how taking this opportunity would align with your financial plan for the future.

3. The other partner makes a compelling case for why they don't think accepting this opportunity is the best choice.

4. What are the alternatives if this career opportunity is not pursued? Discuss what that would look like for both of you.

5. Decide together if you will ask friends and/or family for their viewpoints to see if they have suggestions you might not have considered or if they notice any blind spots. If you agree, talk to them together.

6. As you start moving toward a decision (one partner is starting to see why or why not this opportunity should be snatched up), tune in to how you feel. Do you notice a sense of excitement? A sense of dread? Is part of you shouting, "There has to be another way!"? If you still aren't on the same page, set aside time for renegotiation and revisit the decision-making protocol on page 36 to keep trying to find a win-win.

Discussion Notes

_____

_____

_____

_____

_____

JOB LOSS AND TRANSITION

Naturally, your career paths will have moments of excitement and satisfaction where you are fully committed to your work and valued by your company. However, for any number of reasons, someday you may be faced with job loss, and it's likely that neither of you expected this.

Being let go from a job can leave a person with a profound sense of unfairness. The loss could even lead to depression, making the person who was let go feel immobilized and as if they lack the energy to search for a new job. Naturally, one or both of you will feel anxiety and uncertainty (or fear) around the future. These intense feelings may result in "always saying the wrong thing" or feeling unsupported. Despite these heavy feelings, this is a time when you need to continue building your bond and rise above the calamity as a team. Start discussing now how you can support each other in the face of a job loss or other intense, unexpected transition.

SUPPORT DURING JOB LOSS OR TRANSITION

This is a two-part exercise. First, identify for your partner how to recognize when you might be feeling down or anxious. For example, do you retreat into a dark room and get under the covers? Do you have difficulty waking up in the morning? Do you zone out in front of the television? Do you go for long walks? Include all the things you've noticed you do when you are stressed out, anxious, fearful, sad, and so on; include both helpful and unhelpful default behaviors.

> **PARTNER A**

When I'm feeling down I tend to:

_____

_____

_____

_____

_____

> **PARTNER B**

When I'm feeling down I tend to:

_____

_____

_____

_____

_____

Now, identify for your partner how they can best support you by answering true or false to the statements in the worksheet.

SUPPORTIVE EFFORTS	PARTNER A	PARTNER B
ASK ME HOW I AM DOING AND LISTEN. OFFER ADVICE ONLY IF I ASK.		
BE HONEST WITH ME IF YOU FEEL I AM OVERFOCUSING ON THE ISSUE AND STRESSING YOU OUT.		
GIVE ME SPACE TO HIBERNATE AND RECOUP ON MY OWN BUT CHECK IN WITH ME TO MAKE SURE I'M OKAY.		
MAKE A SPECIAL MEAL FOR ME.		
WATCH A MOVIE OR TELEVISION SHOW WITH ME.		
GIVE ME LOTS OF HUGS AND AFFECTION.		
REACH OUT TO ME FOR SEX.		
SEND ME EMAILS OR TEXTS TO LET ME KNOW YOU ARE THINKING ABOUT ME.		
ENCOURAGE ME WITH MORAL SUPPORT BY REMINDING ME OF WHAT I DO WELL AND OF MY SPECIAL QUALITIES.		

SUPPORTIVE EFFORTS	PARTNER A	PARTNER B
BRAINSTORM WITH ME ABOUT WHAT TO DO NEXT WHEN I ASK FOR HELP.		
GIVE ME A BACKRUB.		
DO NOT JUDGE ME OR FIND REASONS WHY I CAUSED THIS TO HAPPEN.		
ASK ME TO COME TO YOU WHEN I AM READY TO TALK ABOUT WHAT'S GOING ON.		
SET A DATE FOR US TO COME TOGETHER AS A COUPLE TO DECIDE HOW WE WILL MOVE PAST THIS CRISIS.		
ADD YOUR OWN	**PARTNER A**	**PARTNER B**

Partner Discussion

Do you recognize when your partner is feeling down? Did anything they listed surprise you? You don't have to wait for calamity to strike to do the supportive things suggested in this worksheet. Make a note to yourself about what your partner finds supportive. Surprise them with those things even when everything is moving along smoothly.

Discussion Notes

YOUR ROLES AT HOME

One of you might love shopping for the home, keeping the place tidy, and cooking to keep the home fires burning. The other might be career-oriented and on a path to the top-floor corner office. If that's the case, you will have a lovely arrangement. However, if you are both committed to your careers and want a beautiful, clean, well-run home with a fully stocked kitchen, you have some crucial decisions to make as you plan for your future together and keep your home life in good working order.

DIVIDE THE CHORES

Do you like keeping the finances straight and looking for ways to make and save money while your partner enjoys making your home tidy? Keep in mind your natural inclinations as you review what you are willing to take responsibility for around the house. Place a checkmark beside each task you are willing to do or would enjoy doing. It's okay if you both check the same box. It just means that you can do those tasks together.

TASK	PARTNER A	PARTNER B
FUEL AND MAINTAIN CAR		
CLEAN BATHROOM		
CLEAN KITCHEN		
CLEAN BEDROOM		
CLEAN COMMON AREAS		
DECORATE		
DUST AND VACUUM		
EMPTY THE DISHWASHER		
ENTERTAIN (PREPARATIONS FOR)		
GARDEN		
GROCERY SHOP		
DO HOME REPAIRS		

TASK	PARTNER A	PARTNER B
DO LAUNDRY		
PREPARE MEALS		
SET UP SOCIAL CALENDAR		
SHOP FOR HOME GOODS		
SPRING CLEAN		
TAKE CARE OF THE FINANCES (I.E., PAYING BILLS, BALANCING CHECK-BOOK, DOING THE TAXES)		
WASH DISHES		
ADD YOUR OWN	**PARTNER A**	**PARTNER B**

Partner Discussion

Has every chore been accounted for by one or both of you? If not, determine how you will divide the tasks neither of you is particularly interested in. Will you trade off each week or hire someone? Will you exchange the chore for a different one or will a member of your family be willing to help out? Think, too, about what sort of investment, if any, you want to make in things neither of you has time for, like decorating and landscaping.

Discussion Notes

DON'T KEEP SCORE

When you are tired and stressed out, it's easy to feel like your partner is not carrying equal weight. You may find it only natural to say things like, "I am the one who is keeping us afloat" or "I'm the one who spends the most time taking care of the [fill in the blank]." Sometimes you may simply want to feel heard and appreciated. When either of you notices that your partner is complaining of being the one responsible for something, listen to what they're saying and express appreciation for their efforts.

Think of yourselves as a sports team where all players have their positions and each play is intended to bring you closer to winning the game. Assume that each player is doing their best with what they have and what they know. Support your teammate and cheer them on. You're not in competition with your partner. Start your marriage with the assumption that each of you is giving what you can. Find out what's going on and determine how you can support your partner. This may entail reassigning chores.

DISCUSS IMBALANCE IN DUTY AND EFFORT

Issues like this may arise after you've been married for a while, so right now you both might feel you're putting equal effort into your relationship and planning for the future. But be aware that many couples argue over who spends the most time working, who makes the most money, who takes the brunt of the childcare duties, who cleans up, and so on. Don't be surprised if you find yourselves arguing about who does what and who doesn't.

Imagine now that one of you is always cleaning and the other is always working, for instance. Role-play this scenario: The person who is always cleaning resents that the other isn't pulling their weight at home, but the one who is always working feels like they don't have time to clean up around the house because of their work-related responsibilities and exhaustion. You clearly need to have a discussion about any imbalance in duty and effort. Take turns airing your grievance, following this protocol:

1. Determine if this is an issue that really needs to be discussed. Maybe you just need to focus on yourself a bit and engage in some self-soothing. Also ask yourself if your partner is pulling their weight in another area instead of this one. If you still feel the need to discuss this issue, move on to step 2.
2. Ask, "Is now a good time to talk about [fill in the blank]?" If not, agree on a time to discuss the issue.
3. Share your concerns about the imbalance in effort. Share what meaning you are giving to this (such as "you must not care about me"). Name what you are feeling and request a specific alternative.
4. As the partner on the receiving end of this, listen as nondefensively as you can and validate what you heard your partner say by repeating their concern and what they would like to see happen in the future. If you can agree to their request, great. If something is stopping you from being able to do what they would like you to do, explain why you cannot help out in that area or as much as they would like.
5. As the partner with the concern, validate what you heard your partner say. If you understand their point of view, great. If not, suggest a compromise.
6. Brainstorm together until you arrive at a win-win scenario.

Partner Discussion

How did it feel airing your concerns and being on the receiving end, even if it was just a make-believe situation? Did you feel heard? Did you feel defensive? Do you think you can approach this type of discussion in the future without having an argument? Agree that if you ever find yourself feeling like you're doing more than your partner, you will return to this exercise and play it out for real.

Discussion Notes

_____

_____

_____

_____

_____

COUPLE CHECK-IN

Flip back through this chapter and review your responses to the exercises. Were there any sticking points that one or both of you would like to revisit and work on more? What were your three biggest takeaways from this part of the workbook? Take notes in the spaces provided and discuss the items you've listed. Make an agreement to return to the exercises you would like to work further on before moving ahead to the next chapter.

> **PARTNER A**

Exercises I would like to work on more:

_____

_____

_____

_____

_____

My three biggest takeaways were:

1. _____

2. _____

3. _____

> **PARTNER B**

Exercises I would like to work on more:

_____

_____

_____

_____

_____

My three biggest takeaways were:

1. _____

2. _____

3. _____

ACTION ITEMS

1. Visualize an ideal version of your life five years from now. Describe the ideal day to your partner from morning till night. Include where you live, what happens in the morning, when you leave for work, who you interact with, what you are doing, what you do for lunch, what happens when you get home, what you have for dinner, and what you do in the evening to relax and connect.

2. Check out the University of Pennsylvania's Authentic Happiness questionnaire for values in action. (You'll need to register to gain access.) Compare your results to more fully appreciate how your individual jobs match the values you each hold in high regard or determine areas that are out of alignment. (See the Resources section on page 208.) Alternatively, you can do an Internet search for "Work values quiz" and choose among the hits for a quiz you'd both like to take. Compare your answers.

3. Check out career quizzes and aptitude tests on the Internet together to explore how your answers line up with various professions. Do this together so you can each see how the other would respond to the same questions.

4. Role-play going on job interviews with each other. Look up common interview questions on the Internet and take turns playing the role of interviewee and interviewer.

5. If you were independently wealthy and you could have any job in the world, describe to each other what you would do and why, even though you don't need to worry about making money.

CHAPTER

9

Your Future Together

A POWERFUL FORCE HAS brought you together and compelled you to sit down and work conscientiously on building a marriage that will last a lifetime. Before you begin this chapter, I want you to set this workbook aside and spend five minutes sitting across from each other, holding hands and gazing into each other's eyes. Let yourself catch up with the feelings that emerge as you gaze at the person you will soon "have and hold from this day forth." You have already experienced the magic of love. Savor it and let it sink in.

I hope you are feeling a sense of pride in what you have accomplished here. You have stayed the course to learn the strategies, tools, and insights that will help you grow closer together through the years.

MARRIAGE GOALS

You have begun in earnest to map out your goals for your future. I trust that you have found yourselves feeling closer in the process of listening to each other's dreams, hopes, fears, and expectations and have begun to weave them together into a harmonious fabric.

In addition, you have brainstormed how to fit the puzzle pieces of your future together. As you know, the sizes and shapes of those pieces will change throughout the many stages of your life, and challenges will present themselves virtually each step of the way. As you come to this point of pulling together everything you've discussed in this book, I want to underline the intentions that will strengthen the bond between you:

1. Continue to set your aspirations high.
2. Meet each other with earnest and open communication.
3. Bring compassion to each encounter.
4. Validate your appreciation of your partner's feelings along the journey.
5. Be proud of each other's accomplishments.
6. Let your partner know how admiring you are of them.
7. Express gratitude for all the little things your partner does for you.
8. When conflicts arise, treat them as opportunities to learn more about each other.
9. Above all, listen to what matters and what counts to your partner.
10. Take care of yourself so that you can renew the energy to maintain your intentions.

Together you can build an unstoppable team to face anything life may throw at you. Hopefully, by now, your dialogue around common issues and other matters has become a habit. The habit of communicating effectively where you both feel heard and valued will give you the strength you need to make it through any challenges you face.

You will forever have an impact on each other because you will pull for each other to reach for your goals and cheer each other on until you attain them. Always seek to bring out the best in your partner. That's what teammates do. Keep in mind that your partner's influence on you can help you become all that you can be, so be open to that. Being fully known and accepted by another is one of the miracles of the universe. Strive every day to have your partner feel that you are saying "I love you just the way you are."

KEEPING A RECORD OF YOUR GOALS

As you have gathered, creating concrete plans for the future is an ongoing project. My wife and I have a custom that we've enjoyed over the years: In seeking to plan for an abundant life, we come together several times a year to record our thoughts on what that means to each of us. I would like you to do the same.

Choose the times when you will do this. You may choose certain holidays or vacations, or maybe you will do this with each change of season. Purchase a journal that you keep specifically for this purpose. This will be an important keepsake to leave behind for your children, if you decide to have them, and/or a way for you to look over past years and see how far you've come or how your goals have changed.

In your journal, respond to the following prompts each time you come together, allowing for both partners to respond:

1. What have you accomplished since you last checked in on paper? What have you done separately and together that you can look back on with pride?
2. What are five things each of you presently feels grateful for?
3. What challenges are you facing in the near future?
4. What goals do you hope to achieve, both separately and together?
5. Explore the various areas of your life: work, school, relationships with family, children, recreation, travel, friendships, and so on. What can you do to enrich each of those areas?
6. Get out your calendars and start identifying any action steps you can take to reach your goals, including what you want to do and by when.

As you can imagine, this journal will be a sacred record of your journey together. My wife and I have a shelf of many volumes. We started it early in our marriage, 40 years ago. Each time you return to your journal, reread at least your last section. If you've achieved your goals, celebrate them. Laugh at some of the dreams that now seem silly or outdated or have just fallen by the wayside. Maybe you want to rekindle them or maybe you don't. Continue to dream together and keep coming to know each other as fully as possible.

I hope you will continue to cherish and grow your marriage bond and experience much joy throughout the years. May your anniversary celebrations remind you of how hard you have worked and how much fun you have had. May you continue to strengthen your bond as you renew your commitment to be together always.

My very best to you in your future together.

If You Need Further Counseling

I hope you embraced the exercises in this book with gusto and learned new tips and tools to embark on your marriage with confidence.

However, just in case you run into a few snags and begin to wonder if you need additional support, I have included this page to guide you in that decision as well. Here are some reasons to consider seeking a counselor.

1. You find that you push each other's hot buttons on certain topics and you're having difficulty making up in a reasonable time period.
2. The two of you need more help in letting go of past resentments and hurt.
3. You are worried about your partner's alcohol or drug use.
4. You do not always feel safe with your partner when arguments get out of hand.
5. In spite of using these tools and skills, you have a gut feeling that maybe you do not feel sufficient love for your partner and you still feel hesitant to walk down the aisle.
6. Your partner still does not step up to the plate to set a date for your marriage.
7. You have discovered that your partner has had either an emotional or sexual affair. Even if they have expressed remorse, you will want to make sure it does not happen again.

One or more of these concerns will merit the two of you having a discussion about seeking further help.

You can find referrals from several sources—even friends or relatives. Your doctor may have a suggestion. If you feel comfortable with your clergy person or the celebrant at your wedding, you might want to seek a contact there.

You can also go to the American Association for Marriage and Family Therapy to identify a therapist in your area. You will want someone who is either a Clinical Member or a Supervisor and who is licensed in your state.

You may want to interview several to find the one with whom you both feel the best chemistry. Check your health insurance to see if it covers all or a part of the fee.

Resources

BOOKS

Buber, Martin. *I and Thou*. New York: Charles Scribner's Sons, 1970.

Doherty, William J. *The Intentional Family: Simple Rituals to Strengthen Family Ties*. Boston: Addison Wesley, 1999.

Doherty, William J. *Take Back Your Marriage: Sticking Together in a World That Pulls Us Apart*. New York: Guilford Press, 2013.

Glass, Shirley P. *Not "Just Friends": Rebuilding Trust and Recovering Your Sanity After Infidelity*. New York: Free Press, 2004.

Hendrix, Harville. *Getting the Love You Want: A Guide for Couples*. New York: St. Martin's Griffin, 2019.

Hendrix, Harville and Helen Hunt. *Getting the Love You Want Workbook: The New Couples' Study Guide*. New York: Atria, 2003.

Johnson, Sue. *Love Sense: The Revolutionary New Science of Romantic Relationships*. Boston: Little Brown and Company, 2013.

Lofas, Jeanette. *Stepparenting, Everything You Need to Know to Make It Work*. New York: Citadel Press, 2004.

Love, Patricia and Steven Stosny. *How to Improve Your Marriage Without Talking About It*. New York: Harmony Books, 2008.

Paul, Sheryl. *The Conscious Bride: Women Unveil Their True Feelings About Getting Hitched*. California: New Harbinger Publications, 2000.

Perel, Esther. *The State of Affairs: Rethinking Infidelity*. New York: HarperCollins, 2017.

Schwartz, Richard. *You Are the One You've Been Waiting For (Internal Family Systems)*. Illinois: The Center for Self Leadership, 2008.

John Welwood. *Love And Awakening: Discovering The Sacred Path of Intimate Relationships*. New York: Harper Perennial, 1996.

Winfrey, Oprah. *The Wisdom of Sundays: Life-Changing Insights from Super Soul Conversations*. New York: Melcher Media, 2017.

ARTICLES AND WEBSITES

Degges-White, Suzanne. "7 Promises of Intimacy." *Psychology Today*. February 13, 2017. Accessed December 21, 2018. **PsychologyToday.com/us/blog/lifetime -connections/201702/7-promises-intimacy.**

Degges-White, Suzanne. "10 Steps to Effective Couples Communication." *Psychology Today*. May 3, 2016. Accessed December 21, 2018. **PsychologyToday.com/us /blog/lifetime-connections/201605/10-steps-effective-couples-communication.**

EffectiveCommunicationAdvice.com. "10 Tips for Effective Communication for Couples and Marriage." Accessed December 21, 2018. **EffectiveCommunication Advice.com/couples-and-marriage.**

Gordon, Lori H. "Intimacy: The Art of Relationships." *Psychology Today*. Last modified June 9, 2016. Accessed December 21, 2018. **PsychologyToday.com/us /articles/196912/intimacy-the-art-relationships.**

Gottman Institute, The. Subscribe to emails on how to improve your relationship. Accessed December 21, 2018. **Gottman.com/subscribe-blog.**

Graham, Barbara. "How to Improve Your Marriage Without Talking About It." Oprah.com. Accessed December 21, 2018. **Oprah.com/relationships/how-to -improve-your-marriage-without-talking-about-it/all.**

Krull, Erika. "Marriage Communication: 3 Common Mistakes and How to Fix Them." Psych Central. Last modified October 8, 2018. Accessed December 21, 2018. **PsychCentral.com/lib/marriage-communication-3-common-mistakes-and -how-to-fix-them.**

Marriage.com. "Why Intimacy Is Different for Men and Women?" December 26, 2017. Accessed December 21, 2018. **Marriage.com/advice/intimacy/why-intimacy -is-different-for-men-and-women.**

Paquette, Danielle. "Why American Women Are Having Fewer Babies Than Ever." *The Washington Post*. August 16, 2016. Accessed December 21, 2018. **Washington -Post.com/news/wonk/wp/2016/08/16/why-american-women-are-having -fewer-babies-than-ever/?noredirect=on&utm_term=.87f751a96a03.**

Parents.com "Learn About Your Fertility Treatment Options." Accessed December 21, 2018. **Parents.com/getting-pregnant/infertility/treatments /guide-to-fertility-methods.**

Phillips, Lisa A. "The Radical Thrill of Intimacy." *Psychology Today*. Last modified March 8, 2017. Accessed December 21, 2018. **PsychologyToday.com/us /articles/201701/the-radical-thrill-intimacy.**

Quast, Lisa. "10 Tips To Help You Win Every Negotiation." *Forbes*. August 8, 2016. Accessed December 21, 2018. **Forbes.com/sites/lisaquast/2016/08/08/10-tips-to -help-you-win-every-negotiation/#4647e1ff436d.**

Stosny, Steven. "Human Intimacy: Intimacy Is the Essential Lubricant of Humane Behavior." *Psychology Today*. September 14, 2016. Accessed December 21, 2018. **PsychologyToday.com/us/blog/anger-in-the-age-entitlement/201609 /human-intimacy.**

Tartakovsky, Margarita. "7 Persistent Myths About Marriage." PsychCentral. Last modified October 8, 2018. Accessed December 21, 2018. **PsychCentral.com /lib/7-persistent-myths-about-marriage.**

References

Carew Kraft, Jessica. "How Far Apart Should You Space Your Kids?" Forbes. November 8, 2012. Accessed December 21, 2018. **Forbes.com/sites /learnvest/2012/11/08/how-far-apart-should-you-space-your-kids/#64eb7eab1b76.**

Caron, Christina. "Spanking Is Ineffective and Harmful to Children, Pediatricians' Group Says." *The New York Times.* November 5, 2018. Accessed December 21, 2018. **NYTimes.com/2018/11/05/health/spanking-harmful-study-pediatricians.html.**

Chapman, Gary. *The 5 Love Languages: The Secret to Love That Lasts.* Chicago: Northfield Publishing, 2015.

Chapman, Gary. *Things I Wish I Had Known Before We Got Married.* Chicago: Northfield Publishing, 2010.

Cockrell, Clay. "Eight Ways to Keep Your In-Laws Out of Your Marriage." Maritalcounseling.com. July 2, 2015. Accessed December 21, 2018. **MaritalCounseling. com/in-law-problems.**

Cook, Emily. *The Marriage Counseling Workbook: 8 Steps to a Strong and Lasting Relationship.* New York: Althea Press, 2018.

Federal Trade Commission. "Make a Budget." Budget Worksheet. September 2012. Accessed December 21, 2018. **Consumer.gov/sites/www.consumer.gov/files /pdf-1020-make-budget-worksheet_form.pdf.**

Gottman, John M. *The Seven Principles of Making Marriage Work: A Practical Guide by the World's Foremost Relationship Expert.* New York: Harmony Books, 2015.

Happiness Trap, The. "Values Worksheet." Accessed December 21, 2018. **TheHappinessTrap.com/upimages/Values_Questionnaire.pdf.**

Huffington Post. "10 Tips for Managing Your In-laws." December 6, 2017. Accessed December 21, 2018. **HuffingtonPost.com/2014/10/01/in-law-advice_n_5911416.html.**

Johnson, Sue. *Hold Me Tight: Your Guide to the Most Successful Approach to Building Loving Relationships.* New York: Little Brown Spark, 2011.

Lawson, Kimberly. "Why Being Supportive of Your Partner's Career is Essential in a Marriage." Brides. January 17, 2018. Accessed December 21, 2018. **Brides.com /story/why-being-supportive-of-your-partners-career-is-essential-in-a-marriage.**

Mayo Clinic. "Getting Pregnant. Family Planning: Get the Facts About Pregnancy Spacing." February 25, 2017. Accessed December 21, 2018. **MayoClinic.org /healthy-lifestyle/getting-pregnant/in-depth/family-planning/art-20044072?pg=2.**

Newport, Frank. "Five Things We've Learned About Americans and Moral Values." Gallop. June 8, 2015. Accessed December 21, 2018. **News.Gallup.com/opinion /polling-matters/183518/five-things-learned-americans-moral-values.aspx.**

Parent Coach Plan, The. "Parental Responsibilities." Accessed December 21, 2018. **ParentCoachPlan.com/article3.php.**

Ramnarace, Cynthia. "How Couples Can Split Their Money and Bills to Be Fair." Her Money. August 9, 2018. Accessed December 21, 2018. **HerMoney.com/connect/ love/how-couples-can-split-their-money-to-be-fair.**

Rizkalla, Niveen. "Getting Intimate with Intimacy" Tedx Talks. Accessed December 21, 2018. **YouTube.com/watch?v=ydTXf9zp7XE.**

Resolve.org. "Fast Facts." The National Infertility Association. Accessed December 21, 2018. **Resolve.org/infertility-101/what-is-infertility/fast-facts.**

Slotter, Erica B. "Why Your Friends' Approval Is So Crucial to a Relationship." *Psychology Today.* March 13, 2015. Accessed December 21, 2018. **Psychology Today .com/us/blog/me-you-us/201503/why-your-friends-approval-is-so -crucial-relationship.**

WebMD. "Child-Free Living." Accessed December 21, 2018. **WebMD.com /infertility-and-reproduction/child_free_living#1.**

Index

Acknowledgments

I would like to thank the thousands of clients who have trusted me to guide them through the challenges of their relationships. For over 48 years I have learned from them as we collaborated to help them build relationships to last a lifetime.

I want to express appreciation for all of the individuals who have brainstormed with me about ideas for the various topics in this book. My daughter, Elizabeth Curtis, gave me perspective on many of you who might be closer in age to beginning your journey to marriage. She has been a joy in my life.

I want to mention others who have shared their insights: Bob McLennan, Christopher Madson, Gurney Williams III, Janice Hayman, John Holbrook, Martin Buber Alberti, Victoria Sotelo, Victoria Leung, and Wilbert R. Sykes. For the many others who cheered along the sidelines, thanks to you as well.

I appreciate the work of Carol Rosenberg, my developmental editor.

I am especially grateful to my editor, Susan Randol, who trusted that I could write this book. She made many suggestions that guided me toward the book that you have before you. Her assistance was invaluable.

Finally, as you saw in the dedication, I will feel eternally touched by my wife Betsy's deep commitment to encouraging me to create this book. She has given careful and thoughtful consideration to the ideas and the writing. We have grown closer as we worked together to make it happen.

About the Author

For over 40 years, **Jim Walkup** has helped thousands of couples and individuals build meaningful relationships to last a lifetime. He specializes in working with premarital couples and with couples recovering from an extramarital affair. He has been married for 49 years.

He is a licensed marriage and family therapist and has served as president of the New York State Division of Marriage and Family Therapists. In this role, he chaired an organization that seeks to help other marriage and family therapists grow professionally. He is also a Presbyterian minister.

His website, **Dr-Jim.com**, features the popular article "12 Topics You Must Discuss Before Getting Married." By leaving your email address, you can receive other articles about strengthening your marriage. You can reach the author at jimwalkup@gmail.com. He and his wife live in White Plains, New York.

CPSIA information can be obtained
at www.ICGtesting.com
Printed in the USA
JSHW050222060222
22430JS00003B/3